OUSTED!

By
Patrick Keith

MEDIA MA

SINGAP

D1202997

OUSTED! by Patrick Keith
Copyright © 2005 by Media Masters Pte Ltd

Published by:
Media Masters Pte Ltd
Newton Road PO Box 272
Singapore 912210
Email: mediamasters@pacific.net.sg
Website: www.mediamasters.com.sg

Lay-out & Design by O'Art, Singapore
Printed by Mui Kee Press & Company, Singapore

First published July 2005

ISBN 981-05-3865-0

FOREWORD

Singapore's ejection from the Federation of Malaysia will forever be of immense historical importance to the two territories involved. This is undeniable. That the events recalled here will long impact on matters of South East Asian security, stability, economic progress and cross-cultural understanding, similarly, cannot be challenged.

Why then, it is appropriate to ask, has it taken four decades for a book like this to become available to the general public?

The answer is deceptively simple: its subject matter.

Any local author or publisher considering a book project of this nature would have immediately felt encumbered by two correlated factors – the need for self-censorship and the risk of courting the wrath of key political camps involved during this turbulent period. Pointedly, the same political power structures operating 40 years ago, in essence, remain in place today.

Forty years ago I was following a career path as Deputy Director of External Information within the Malaysian government apparatus. In this capacity I was able to follow and experience, at extremely close quarters, the rage and bitterness being generated on both sides of the Causeway. The intensity of the wrangling, time and again, superseded the very issues up for resolution.

As a number of politicians have led the way by providing, naturally enough, their specific takes on these events, I felt the time had come to attempt a different way of approaching the separation story. There has been, after all, a dramatic maturing of political consciousness in both Singapore and Malaysia over the past four decades and, without question, history demands this story be related from more than one angle.

Patrick Keith
Melbourne
July, 2005

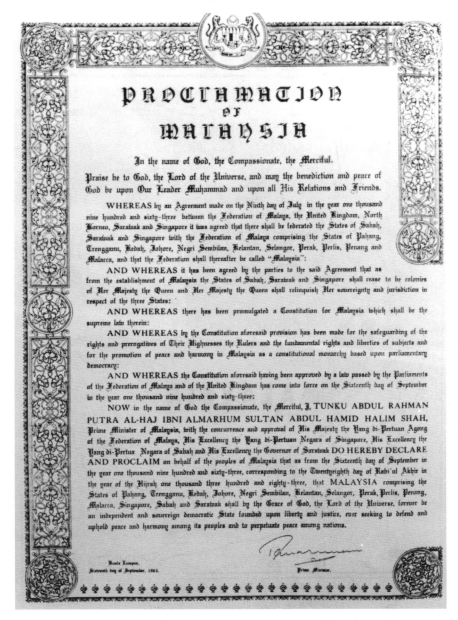

PROCLAMATION
OF
MALAYSIA

In the name of God, the Compassionate, the Merciful.

Praise be to God, the Lord of the Universe, and may the benediction and peace of God be upon Our Leader Muhammad and upon all His Relations and Friends.

WHEREAS by an Agreement made on the Ninth day of July in the year one thousand nine hundred and sixty-three between the Federation of Malaya, the United Kingdom, North Borneo, Sarawak and Singapore it was agreed that there shall be federated the States of Sabah, Sarawak and Singapore with the Federation of Malaya comprising the States of Pahang, Trengganu, Kedah, Johore, Negri Sembilan, Kelantan, Selangor, Perak, Perlis, Penang and Malacca, and that the Federation shall thereafter be called "Malaysia":

AND WHEREAS it has been agreed by the parties to the said Agreement that as from the establishment of Malaysia the States of Sabah, Sarawak and Singapore shall cease to be colonies of Her Majesty the Queen and Her Majesty the Queen shall relinquish Her sovereignty and jurisdiction in respect of the three States:

AND WHEREAS there has been promulgated a Constitution for Malaysia which shall be the supreme law therein:

AND WHEREAS by the Constitution aforesaid provision has been made for the safeguarding of the rights and prerogatives of Their Highnesses the Rulers and the fundamental rights and liberties of subjects and for the promotion of peace and harmony in Malaysia as a constitutional monarchy based upon parliamentary democracy:

AND WHEREAS the Constitution aforesaid having been approved by a law passed by the Parliaments of the Federation of Malaya and of the United Kingdom has come into force on the Sixteenth day of September in the year one thousand nine hundred and sixty-three:

NOW in the name of God the Compassionate, the Merciful, I, TUNKU ABDUL RAHMAN PUTRA AL-HAJ IBNI ALMARHUM SULTAN ABDUL HAMID HALIM SHAH, Prime Minister of Malaysia, with the concurrence and approval of His Majesty the Yang di-Pertuan Agong of the Federation of Malaya, His Excellency the Yang di-Pertuan Negara of Singapore, His Excellency the Yang di-Pertua Negara of Sabah and His Excellency the Governor of Sarawak DO HEREBY DECLARE AND PROCLAIM on behalf of the peoples of Malaysia that as from the Sixteenth day of September in the year one thousand nine hundred and sixty-three, corresponding to the Twentyeighth day of Rabi'ul Akhir in the year of the Hijrah one thousand three hundred and eighty-three, that MALAYSIA comprising the States of Pahang, Trengganu, Kedah, Johore, Negri Sembilan, Kelantan, Selangor, Perak, Perlis, Penang, Malacca, Singapore, Sabah and Sarawak shall by the Grace of God, the Lord of the Universe, forever be an independent and sovereign democratic State founded upon liberty and justice, ever seeking to defend and uphold peace and harmony among its peoples and to perpetuate peace among nations.

Kuala Lumpur,
Sixteenth day of September, 1963.

Prime Minister.

The official document formally sealing the union of Malaya, Singapore and the Borneo territories of Sabah and Sarawak into a single Federation of Malaysia.

Contents

SECTION 1

The Prince and the Ghostly Snake 9

The Envelope Affair 19

Alliance for Independence 27

Red Ribbons on a Silver Platter 35

To Hell with Sukarno 43

Riots from Indonesia 55

Stab in the Back 63

A New Storm 69

SECTION 2

The Trapped Lion 79

The PAP Trounced 89

Blood Must Flow 95

The Unspoken Word 105

The 'Ultras' 117

The Unbending Backbone 127

SECTION 3

The Man from Malacca 137

Confronting Lee Kuan Yew 145

Dealing with the Wreckers 151

The Fight Goes on 159

A to Z and Z to A 167

The Josey Affair 171

Destination Disaster 179

The Final Act 185

Happy and hopeful days for then Malayan leader, Tunku Abdul Rahman and his Singapore counterpart, Lee Kuan Yew. This picture was taken in July, 1962, when 10,000 well-wishers thronged Singapore's airport to wish the Tunku a safe and successful journey to London for continuing talks on the lead-up to Malaysia.

SECTION 1

Tunku Abdul Rahman, born into Malay royalty, spent much of his youth in Britain. Later in life, back in Malaya, he became a reluctant politician. Thereafter he was driven by the belief that history would judge him both a great leader and protector of his people. The following chapters portray the Tunku's perspective on the separation story.

The Prince and the Ghostly Snake

The Envelope Affair

Alliance for Independence

Red Ribbons on a Silver Platter

To Hell with Sukarno

Riots from Indonesia

Stab in the Back

A New Storm

One from the author's private album. Patrick Keith is shown here chatting with the Tunku. This picture was taken in the late 1950s.

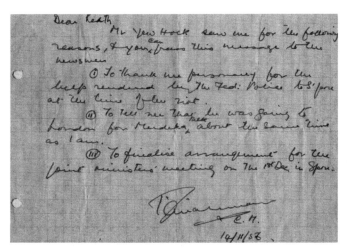

A sample of the numerous personal notes and instructions from the Tunku received by the author during his government service days. The text reads:

Dear Keith

Mr Yew Hock saw me for the following reasons, and you can pass this message to the newsmen.

To thank me personally for the help rendered by the Fed. Police to S'pore at the time of the riot.

To tell me that he was going to London for Merdeka talks about the same time as I am.

To finalise arrangement for the joint ministers' meeting on the 1st Dec in Singapore.

8

THE PRINCE AND
THE GHOSTLY SNAKE

In late June, 1965, Tunku Abdul Rahman, Prime Minister of Malaysia, was resting in his suite in London's swank Ritz Hotel. He was suffering from a debilitating bout of shingles. Despite the pain, he spent time reviewing numerous unsettling reports from home.

The Tunku had originally travelled to Britain to attend that year's Commonwealth Prime Ministers' Conference. The shingles had resulted in his absence from several important sessions.

Well recognised back home as 'the Prince who enjoyed the Good Life,' the Malaysian leader nevertheless was also one for respecting the duties of high office. He had held out bravely against worsening pain to present his arguments before the gathering of his peers. He also made sure he had been on hand for two significant social obligations. The first of these was a day with British Prime Minister Harold Wilson at Chequers; the second, a visit with Commonwealth Relations Secretary Arthur Bottomley at Doonybrook.

The Tunku was also a thoughtful husband who confided in a couple of trusted journalists travelling in his party that he wished to avoid unsettling Puan Sharifah Rodziah in Kuala Lumpur. His spouse was a worrier and he was fearful she might panic on news of his sickness and catch the first London-bound plane. Which was exactly what happened.

By the time the Prime Ministers' Conference ended on June 25, the shingles had worsened and the Tunku missed the banquet for visiting Commonwealth leaders given by the Queen at Buckingham

Palace. On June 26, he was at the London Clinic, reading Queen Elizabeth II's consoling note, wishing him a quick recovery.

The setback in his health put the otherwise cheerful leader in an uncharacteristically reflective mood.

Back in Malaysia, news of his hospitalisation was received with alarm. It was particularly worrying for the superstitious who believed the viral disease was the work of some evil spirit. A ghostly snake was believed to be the cause of shingles. Its malevolent spirit roamed the world seeking an opportunity to stifle an innocent person. Usually striking a man in the middle of his back, the ghostly snake then worked outwards to the right and left, trying to curl itself around his waist. The superstition would have it that death resulted when the two ends were allowed to meet at the victim's navel.

In days gone by, drastic measures were taken to save lives from ghostly snakes. The village medicine-man was summoned at once. He would dutifully and ceremoniously arrive with a bowl of burning incense, the petals of seven different flowers, water from seven different rivers and all the other paraphernalia of his trade. As the rest of the gathering recited prayers, he chanted his mantras and invoked spirits stronger than that of the snake's. In the meantime, the patient was stripped and his waist closely examined to establish the exact positions of the snake's head and its tail. The medicine-man, guided by his magical powers, decided when to scorch both ends of the reptile with a burning ember or some fiery acid. The patient could be left with agonizing burns but the exercise was another triumph over an evil spirit. The man would be scarred; but he was alive!

Malaysia's prime minister would rather chuckle at ancient superstitions. As a betting man, he preferred risking his chips on modern medicine. Fifteen years of studying and gallivanting in Britain as a youth had gained him a reasonable respect for science. At the London Clinic in 1965, he was assured of quality care but the Tunku was worried about issues far, far bigger than shingles.

He had come to the London conference with two main objectives – to warn the other 'Commonwealth club' leaders of the growing danger in Vietnam and to ask them to stand more solidly behind Malaysia against Indonesian aggression.

Apart from being taken ill, the Tunku was finding this London trip unquestionably annoying and difficult. At the recently concluded conference, he had run into a small group of cocky leaders from Africa who showed little respect for their more senior colleagues. They had no time for the growing menace in Vietnam and did not want to hear about it. Certainly not from someone like the Tunku whom they regarded as old-fashioned in his political outlook.

Neither were they interested in the problems of Malaysia. They took the attitude that Malaysia should have known better than to get into a row with Indonesia's sabre-rattling President Sukarno who cast a giant shadow on the world stage.

The Tunku's patience was sorely tried. It occurred to him that his fellow Commonwealth leaders chose to forget how he had once stuck his neck out for Africa. On the morning of March 22, 1960, he had been appalled at newspaper pictures of the Sharpeville massacre in South Africa. Dozens of men and women, demonstrating peacefully outside a police station, had been mown down with rifle and machine-gun fire. The same day, at the Malaysian Parliament, he had delivered an impassioned attack against the vileness of apartheid. Two months later, at the 1960 Prime Ministers' Conference in London, he had kicked up such a fuss that his stinging rebuke of apartheid helped force South Africa out of the Commonwealth.

Nobody seemed to remember all that in 1965. But that was life, with its shingles and ingratitude and brash young men who thought they knew the answer to every problem. The Tunku silently mourned the passing of a more gracious era. Much younger members now strutted about, their inflated self-confidence and unremitting self-importance destroying the old brotherly atmosphere which used to prevail at previous Commonwealth meetings.

Fortunately, life also had its consolations. The weather outside was London at its best. His room was filled with baskets of flowers, and flowers meant friends. But better than friends was his dear wife. It was good to have her soothing presence around. He remembered with grateful affection that in his first years in politics, she had served him, cooked and washed for him, without complaint. She was a quiet lovable person and he had no complaints, though he sometimes wished she would try a little harder to keep her weight down.

The weight issue was one of the Tunku's favourite topics for private, gentle jokes. Once, on a visit to Bangkok, he was interviewed on radio. "Tunku," the reporter asked, "do you have a message for the people back home or for your family?" The leader chuckled into the microphone and replied: "Yes, I want to send this message to my wife. I'm doing fine but don't you eat too much while I'm away. You're fat as it is and I don't want you to get even fatter." This message, delivered with no malice and in good humour, was heard and enjoyed by the whole nation. Nobody in Malaya would ever accuse the Tunku of being deliberately unkind.

Fat or otherwise, it was comforting to have her with him in London and it made the agony of shingles a little more bearable. He could do little, except read the London dailies and they invariably added to his distress. The front pages were filled with news about Ratna Sari Dewi, the former Japanese barmaid who had become Sukarno's fourth wife. Dewi was now visiting Europe in lavish style. In France, pages and pages were devoted to large photographs accompanying reports on her flamboyance. It was similar in Britain. Dewi was hot copy and sold papers. The fact that the Malaysian prime minister was sick was dismissed in one or two paragraphs in the inside pages.

The Tunku knew enough of the world to recognise that an old man's shingles was no match to a youthful pretty face evoking large whiffs of scandal in high places. Still, he felt he deserved better. He was, after all, the prime minister of a friendly Commonwealth country fighting together with Britain in a war against Indonesia. Malaysian and British troops had been killed in that war, and here was the British press slighting him and pampering Sukarno's woman.

If this were an isolated case of bad treatment by the British press, the Tunku would have merely filed it in his phenomenal memory for slights, to be drawn out only when it was called for. But it appeared to him now that, over the previous months, British newsmen had been giving him a raw deal. Where they had then been merely unfriendly, they had now turned blatantly unfair. The Malaysian politician found it difficult to understand the reason for this undercurrent of antagonism. He had always been a close friend of Britain, despite some unpleasant experiences which could easily have turned him against the drastically diminished empire. Of these, two stood out in the Tunku's memory.

At 16, the Tunku was admitted to St Catharine's College at Cambridge where he decided to lodge. He was informed there was a waiting list. Rooms were limited and could only be granted on rotation. The young prince from Kedah in northern Malaya thought the explanation was reasonable enough and waited. However, the waiting list appeared endless. Sensing something was amiss, the student went up to the dean and asked why, after three long years, he had not been allocated a room. The reply was direct and succinct: "This college was built for English gentlemen. I can't let you stay here because I know the British gentlemen won't like it."

Stunned, he recalled the affront in a letter to his family in Kedah. The Sultan was furious and promptly dispatched his British adviser to London to convey formally his displeasure over the treatment of his son. The trip produced immediate results. The dean at St Catharine's sent for the Malay prince and apologized. Of course, a room was now available. Did he wish to move in straightaway?

The Kedah royal rejected the offer. Recounting the unfortunate episode years later, he explained: "I didn't want to be allotted a room simply because my father was a sultan. I wanted it understood that all students from Malaya should be treated fairly." Nearly 50 years after the experience, the Tunku would claim it to be his first lesson in patriotism: "From that moment on, I decided to work for freedom from British rule."

There was a second major example of shabby, discriminatory treatment the Tunku had kept in his 'slight file'. It happened in 1955 as Malaya was moving inexorably towards independence. The Alliance Party, headed by the Tunku, had won 51 of the 52 available seats in the Federal Legislative Council. It was, by all accounts, a stunning election victory that established the Kedah prince as the only local political leader to be reckoned with.

He became Chief Minister, an office that should have come with certain privileges, like the use of a government car and an official residence. The British, hanging on tenuously to their claim on Malaya, failed to provide him with a car. When they assigned him a house, it was of the type usually given to fairly junior officials in the colonial service. When the Tunku turned it down, the alternative was a much larger wooden house, but in a sad state of disrepair. It was so bad, in fact, that when it rained, there was a mad scramble for buckets to collect the water that came cascading through various sections of the roof.

It rankled. The Tunku was well aware of how different his situation was from the British who lived nearby. He knew that, in adjoining suburbs, convenient cocoons existed, protecting select groups of civil servants and businessmen who appeared oblivious that their privileged days in Malaya were distinctly numbered. They lived in air-conditioned luxury and spent hours in their exclusive *for whites only* clubs, indulging in flippant conversations and passing disdainful remarks about the lowly locals over countless mugs of beer or copious shots of whisky and soda. They returned to rooms with huge armchairs and chintz-covered cushions, homes maintained meticulously, thanks to an army of uniformed servants. They employed cooks, cleaning women, gardeners, chauffeurs and an assortment of odd-job 'boys'.

Among the imposing homes that were a stark contrast to the official residence of Malaya's first chief minister was the abode of the British High Commissioner in Malaya, still the highest authority in the land. The mansion was a commanding presence on a hill that had an enviable view of the grand bungalows below. Sir Donald MacGillivray was the complete opposite of his predecessor, General Sir Gerald Templer. MacGillivray was a gentle, soft-spoken man who appeared to understand and sympathize with the increasingly strident demands for independence and was actually helping pave the way for it. Astute political observers could say he had little choice. After just on seven years of fighting the Communist Party of Malaya (CPM) and failing to destroy its hard-core leadership, Her Majesty's Government was seeking a decent way out of its Malayan predicament. But how could they withdraw without losing face? How could they submit to calls for independence without losing the dignity that had been accorded them as a colonial power? No matter. On stormy nights, as pails slowly filled with rainwater at the Tunku's house, the kindly MacGillivray in his mansion on the hill, surrounded by armed guards, lay in lofty comfort and slept undisturbed.

For the Tunku, those unnecessarily inconvenient nights in 1955 summed up another major slight he had to endure in the struggle for Malaya's independence. Lying in bed, disturbed by the din of water splashing in buckets, he swore he would do everything in his power to end British rule sooner than the colonials would have it. The decrepit house the British had assigned him would one day give way to the magnificent headquarters of the Malaysian Ministry of Foreign Affairs. At the opening ceremony, the Tunku, after whom the new site would be named, spoke and, in his musings, recalled the wooden house of many leaks, the sudden tropical storms and the essential buckets.

There were other incidents which could have made him bitter but the Tunku was the master of his emotions. He was also a virtuoso at turning negative experiences to his eventual advantage. He chose what to feel and when. He would not allow his daily reactions to life be dictated to by the circumstances surrounding him.

Haste, as far as the Tunku was concerned, resulted in errors of judgement and mistakes meant misspent energy. Better to take one's time and arrive at decisions when one was not rushed, or pressured. Keep a cool head; it was a man's best friend. A cool head meant less regrets and less regrets made for a congenial existence. What for was life? Thus, the episode at Cambridge left the memory of an obsequious dean at St Catharine's, a man put in his place in a country that put so much stock in the structure of the classes. Still, in a way, it had added to the Tunku's enjoyment of England. In much the same way, the leaking roof at his first official residence did not stop him being gracious to the later British leaders in Malaya who did not exactly endear themselves to him. And when independence came, the Tunku chose to maintain the closest possible friendship with Britain.

He gave the British full credit for their contribution to Malaya's progress, going against the fashion of the day when governments of newly-independent countries went out of their way to twist the tail of the British lion to show they were not stooges. Within the Tunku's Alliance Party, there were a number of boisterous men who would have eagerly taken the same route had he not held them firmly in check.

The Tunku resisted all attempts to seek a closer relationship with new friends in Asia and Africa at the expense of Britain and older friends in the Commonwealth. Under his leadership, British interests in Malaya were treated with the highest respect and consideration. He paid no attention to derogatory remarks about his stance. He refused to tolerate attempts to undermine his decisions to accommodate or cooperate. He was convinced his position would redound to Malaya's benefit. The Tunku had acquired a deep respect for the British principles of parliamentary democracy, the concept of the rule of law and the British judicial system. He was determined to make them work in independent Malaya.

Even at the time of the Suez affair in 1956, when British forces overran the Egyptian army in Suez, the Malayan leader had resisted all pressure to turn against Britain. Large sections of his own predominantly-Muslim party were in a dangerous mood over the invasion by 'infidels' and were demanding Malaya take an anti-British stand. But the Tunku stubbornly refused to join in any public rebuke of an old friend who was facing abuse from all over the world.

The Tunku's style of friendship was sometimes a political liability and made him a target of vicious and damaging attacks even in Malaya. Later, Sukarno was to use it in his world-wide propaganda effort to portray the Tunku as a British 'stooge'. However, the Malay prince held firmly to his conviction that genuine friendship was a thing of immeasurable value and should be preserved, whatever the cost.

By mid-1965 this conviction was being tested. In spite of the Tunku's friendship and warm feelings for Britain, many London newspapers had been giving him a bad press. They had been attacking him over his handling of domestic affairs, particularly in regard to Singapore. The reports portrayed a bungling, ineffectual leader who could not – or worse, would not – control the extremists in his party. They implied he was failing to understand the nature of the forces at work in Malaysia. On the other hand, British reporters were projecting Lee Kuan Yew, Prime Minister of Singapore, as a man of genius, a dynamic, efficient leader who could do a far better job of Malaysia if he had the chance. Even worse for the Tunku, several American and Australian newspapers had begun to follow the British line.

December 28, 1955. The Tunku, together with Singapore Chief Minister David Marshall and MCA President Tan Cheng Lock, walks to a preliminary press conference to the Baling peace talks. Later in life the Tunku would describe his Baling negotiations with Communist Party of Malaya (CPM) leaders thus :

"The only good thing The Emergency produced was my meeting with Chin Peng. Because of those talks of mine in Baling, we were able to wrest the initiative from the Malayan Communist Party, then sit at a conference table in London to negotiate our independence with the British, and win our freedom as a nation. Baling led straight to Merdeka."

Cooped up at the London Clinic the Tunku wondered if Britain realised that no friendship, however strong, could survive the kind of beating his Alliance Party leadership was getting. He had been reminded by British advisers on many occasions that the press in England was free and if reporters became critical, there was nothing the government could do about it. He had also been assured that press opinion in the country did not always reflect the attitude and policies of the British government.

The Tunku called such advice and assurances to mind as he lay in his sickbed but wasn't appeased. He had studied the recent attacks very closely and found it impossible to escape the conclusion that some of it had been inspired or engineered by British officials. It was equally difficult to dispel the feeling that behind a number of these attacks on him in foreign newspapers lurked a non-British figure – the figure of Lee Kuan Yew, leader of Singapore's ruling People's Action Party (PAP).

Every now and then, despite himself, the Tunku overlooked the flowers that graced his room and would not be soothed by the constant flow of warm messages from friends. In late June, 1965, so many disturbing things had already transpired in Malaysia and these presently kept him preoccupied. The images that now crowded his mind were of infinite significance to the future of Malaysia.

Tunku Abdul Rahman, master of his emotions, was being called upon to react. Once the shingles had subsided and he could move his legs without wrenching pain, he began mulling over the events of the past few years and weighing the various episodes in his mind. Then he started to jot down his thoughts, splitting them into columns that would, in the end, run into several fullscap pages. It was characteristic of the way he approached the issues he wanted to settle once and for all. Slowly and surely, he began to fashion the tragic decision that would make brilliant men weep in anger.

THE ENVELOPE AFFAIR

The Tunku never forgot that Lee Kuan Yew had been a most persistent and persuasive advocate of the proposal for the merger between Malaya and Singapore. He claimed the Singapore leader had kept pressing home his case quietly but irresistibly, with easy skill and charm and the right touch of deference. The Singapore politician's pursuit was relentless, said the Tunku. He lobbied on the golf course, across the poker table, over meals, at cocktail parties. "Lee never let up," the Tunku would recall many years after the ouster of Singapore from the Federation in 1965. "He was in my sitting room, my dining room and even my bedroom, morning, noon and night. He wouldn't let me sleep until I agreed to the merger."

Lee's persistence was not the only reason for the merger, and certainly not the main one. It was obvious the British had no desire to be in the forefront of another protracted showdown with the communists, this time staged in a prominent trading port; another costly battle that would surely court more international attention. There was also the case of the North Borneo states, Sabah and Sarawak. They remained undeveloped despite years of colonial rule and their exploitative value to Britain had largely diminished. England had to find her way out of that situation too. Her representatives in Malaya needed to work overtime.

There had been no respite to British reminders to the Tunku about the communist threat and Singapore's plight. After containing the CPM strength in Malaya largely by paying vast sums of money to exhausted CPM 'commanders', the Tunku, on his part, had been watching with increasing anxiety the steady growth of communist influence on the neighbouring island. The threat there was proving more insidious, obviously directed by men who were better schooled and politically more astute than the CPM leadership he had met at Baling nearly a decade earlier. He had inveigled and entrapped those naïve, surprisingly trusting jungle fighters and used his two-day meeting with them as a propaganda ploy and, ultimately, bargaining chips in London where in the first hours of 1956 he flew to argue the case for Malayan independence.

Singapore in the beginning of the Sixties was a different picture. It seemed to the Tunku that there was a real danger communism could take hold on the island and soon capture power. In the Tunku's opinion, Lee had tried to be a little too clever at one stage, believing he could make use of the communists to fight the British and then discard them when the struggle for freedom had been won. Other men like him had mounted the communist tiger but finished up in its stomach, and Lee, in the Malayan leader's view, was already half-way down its throat.

If it had been Lee's future alone that was at stake, the Tunku would not have interfered. He would have been sorry to see the decline, perhaps even the political demise, of a young man of such brilliance and promise. But the interests of Singapore were another matter. The endless bickering among the island's leaders made him nervous. He found it difficult to follow the high-sounding political exchanges. In any case the Tunku regarded the constant heated talk quite irrelevant. He was more concerned about the mood that pervaded on the ground. The chronic work unrest, the incessant strikes gave Singapore the sombre air of unrelieved crisis.

The Tunku would have preferred to leave the island alone, but he could not accept the possibility of a communist success there. A communist-dominated Singapore was unthinkable. It would inevitably become a 'second Cuba', a base for subverting Malaya and other countries in the region. To prevent this he had to help save Singapore from communism and this could be achieved only by merging the island with Malaya. The merger would in turn save Lee from his communist rivals.

This was not an easy task. There were many men in the Tunku's United Malays National Organisation (UMNO) who were vehemently opposed to the proposed merger for simple mathematical reasons.

This was how they viewed merger: In Malaya, the Malays slightly outnumbered the immigrant Chinese. They felt safe under the protection of the police and the armed forces which were overwhelmingly Malay. On the other hand, Singapore was predominantly Chinese. In the event of a merger, the Chinese would easily outnumber the Malays. In such changed circumstances, a Malay contemplating the future would feel his heretofore special place in society threatened. He would become acutely aware that the Chinese were miles ahead of the Malays in both education and economics. The Chinese owned most of the shops and made more money. Already they held most of the economic power in Malaya. If their numbers increased, where would the Malays stand? UMNO leaders, vehemently against merger, painted dire scenarios.

The British came up with an ingenious solution that would enable them to escape from the region without losing face. Within this scheme they could pass their responsibility for cleaning up the CPM mess to former subjects who, in turn, would hopefully go all out to prove they were worthy of independence. Britain still had two other colonies in the area – British North Borneo (Sabah) and Sarawak – and a British protectorate, the little oil-rich state of Brunei. These territories had become increasingly a source of embarrassment. The days of colonialism were clearly over and, in any case, Sabah and Sarawak were no longer of much value. A way had to be found to grant them freedom. Simply to withdraw and leave them on their own would have meant abandoning them to Indonesia's President Sukarno. Clearly, they were too small and weak to stand by themselves. Britain could not afford to be seen on the international stage as a ruthless colonial divesting herself of still backward real estate she had mercilessly exploited.

If Malaya could be persuaded to accept them, together with Singapore, in a larger federation, Britain could make the gracious exit she needed.

Britain's proposition appealed to the Tunku. Sabah and Sarawak had sizeable native populations. They were not Malay, but by adroit manipulation they could be made to side with the Malays against the Chinese. The tiny state of Brunei was almost completely Malay. Together, they could help offset Singapore's Chinese population.

Thus, the plan for Malaysia came about; a new nation to be made up of Malaya, Singapore, Sabah, Sarawak and Brunei. Later, as the plan got more refined, the Sultan of Brunei began to perceive that the rest were interested in his state for its money more than for itself, and decided to opt out of the federation. In Sabah and in Sarawak, the initial hasty outbursts against the Malaysia plan quickly changed to support when the leaders were warned of the rapacious gleam in Sukarno's eyes. They were convinced that if they stayed out of Malaysia they would soon be gobbled up by Indonesia.

The Tunku would later reveal that once he agreed to go ahead with the Malaysia plan, he noted a dramatic change in Lee Kuan Yew. The old charm was rapidly replaced by a strutting cockiness. The deference the Singapore leader had once shown his Malayan counterpart was superseded by a defiant attitude. Lee, the Tunku said, began displaying the arrogance of a man supremely confident that he was the intellectual giant in the land. UMNO's strong men claimed this unbridled display of brilliance made Lee look ridiculous at times. They disliked him more because he appeared to be dazzled by his own performance. They would not admit that they themselves were dazzled.

The first shock to the Tunku came during the negotiations on the financial arrangements for Singapore's entry into Malaysia. Singapore was wealthy, with over $400 million* in reserve and the merger promised even greater prosperity. The Tunku had agreed that the island should become the 'New York' of Malaysia while Kuala Lumpur would be the seat of government, the 'Washington DC.' In Singapore, a vast new industrial estate was already being carved out in Jurong to accommodate the new industries which would flock to the island to take advantage of the proposed Malaysian common market. Singapore businessmen were excited at the prospects ahead.

Singapore was easily the most advanced of the states that would form Malaysia. She had the highest rate of literacy, the highest standard of living and the highest per capita income, second only to Japan in Asia. Above all this, it was better equipped than the other states to take advantage of the new opportunities Malaysia would bring.

On the other hand, the mainstream of regional progress had largely by-passed Sabah and Sarawak, both badly hampered by colonial neglect. In the remote, inaccessible backlands of Sarawak, head-hunters had only recently begun to emerge into the world of the 20th century. There were few schools and even fewer hospitals. The general level of income was low although the vast timberlands of Sabah, home of massive trees, had created many millionaires and paid handsome dividends in London. The British were leaving the two territories with backward economic and social set-ups, and both would need massive injections of aid if they were to be lifted to the levels of other states in the future federation.

It seemed only fair to the Tunku that wealthy Singapore should contribute its share in this expensive undertaking. Lee Kuan Yew was asked if his government would be generous enough to make an outright grant of $50 million*. He turned it down flatly and was only prepared, after a lot of very unpleasant haggling, to offer a loan on special terms. The Tunku said the Singapore leader was not content with winning this argument. Lee, he claimed, had begun to make unfair charges and threats against Malaya and to make them in public. He accused the Malayan Finance Minister, Tan Siew Sin, of trying to loot Singapore, of having malicious intentions against the island. According to the Tunku he was warned by Lee that Malaysia would collapse if force was used to take away Singapore's reserves and that the island's population would not be cowed even if the entire Malayan army was stationed within its boundaries.

The notorious 'one per cent affair' also occurred around this time and it, too, nearly wrecked the Malaysia plan.

As its share of the annual cost of Malaysia, Singapore was asked to contribute 55 per cent of the federal revenue collected within the island. Lee found this figure too high. Anxious for an early agreement to be reached, the Tunku agreed to knock it back to 40 per cent. Lee bargained further and wanted it pegged at 39 per cent and was said to have kicked up a monumental fuss, not just in Kuala Lumpur, but all the way to London where talks were being held with the British government on the Malaysia Agreement.

By this time the Tunku had begun to feel Lee was going too far. It was not just the one per cent argument that bothered him. It was Lee's whole attitude to Malaysia. The Tunku perceived the Singaporean was determined to grab as much as he could while giving as little as possible in return. The nitpicking bothered him and the Malay prince was known for his dislike of fiddly attitudes that marred associations and relationships. The Tunku felt strongly that unless the rich states were willing to share their prosperity with the poorer ones, Malaysia would stand on shaky foundations. He decided there could be no compromise on this and sent a message to the Malaysian delegation in London to break off talks if Lee refused to budge.

There were other such squabbles. 'The Historic Envelope' episode truly rankled with the Tunku for a long, long time.

Before leaving for London to take part in the final negotiations on the Malaysia Agreement, Lee had announced: "I am ready to squat it out as long as anyone else. I am prepared to talk till the cows come home." He was true to his word. His relentless bargaining, hour after hour, reduced most of the other delegates to mental and physical exhaustion. One session went from early evening till dawn.

Just when the Tunku thought all issues had been ironed out, Lee asked to include an additional condition to the loan which Singapore would provide for development projects in Sabah and Sarawak. He wanted 50 per cent of the labour for these projects to come from Singapore. The Tunku agreed to it readily, for apart from his anxiety to get the matter out of the way as soon as possible, it seemed a reasonable demand in view of Singapore's unemployment problem. But Lee, the Tunku remembered, was not satisfied with only a verbal assurance. He argued to have it in writing and urged the Tunku to sign it.

Long afterwards, the Tunku would confide how he had steeled himself as he listened to the Singapore leader's plea for a written confirmation. He said he was filled with disgust. What sort of man was this who would refuse to accept his word and insist on getting his signature? No-one had ever demeaned him in this manner before.

So, a 'document' had to be drawn up. The 'agreement' was scribbled on the back of an envelope Lee grabbed from a side table in the sitting room of the Tunku's Ritz Hotel suite, venue for their private talks.

The Tunku said he could hardly conceal his contempt at the 'document'. He scanned it briefly and signed it with a flourish.

Lee Kuan Yew must have felt satisfied clutching that envelope. He was not to know it would forever be remembered as the first instance that really earned him the Tunku's personal disaffection. Not the refusal of the $50 million* grant, not the one per cent argument. These were just annoying incidents the Kedah prince could have dismissed as the sort of occupational hazards politicians accepted on sufferance.

It was the 'grubby envelope' that hit a raw nerve. It proved to the Tunku that the PAP leader had his own agenda and would, in all likelihood, jeopardize the Sino-Malay-Indian unity he had been nursing in the peninsula. It was a personal affront and the Tunku found it impossible to chuckle about it even after years and years. It was the insult that made the prince think he must protect his Alliance men against the abrasive ambitions of his neighbour. Men like Lee, the Tunku began thinking on that day at the Ritz, should be treated at arm's length, like guests in one's home. See to their needs; look after their comfort. But they should also be watched and if they crossed the line, they should be made to realise they have overstayed their welcome.

From day one, you might say, the UMNO leader had his misgivings but was still determined to make Malaysia work. Though – not at all costs.

---

* Currency references throughout this book are in Straits dollars.

August 31, 1957. The final ceremonial lowering of the British flag in Kuala Lumpur; an act symbolizing the end of a colonial era.

Dato Onn bin Jaafar, the founding president of the United Malay National Organisation (UMNO), a man whose bright political star was suddenly eclipsed in the mid-1950s after he had attempted to re-organise the party along non-racial lines.

ALLIANCE FOR INDEPENDENCE

On August 31, 1963, Malaya celebrated its sixth year as an independent nation. Six happy and exciting years had gone by since the first *Merdeka* Day celebrations. For Tunku Abdul Rahman, nothing would compare with the jubilation of 1957.

On the night of August 30, 1957, the Tunku had joined the huge crowds which turned out in Kuala Lumpur to welcome *Merdeka*. Freedom! They assembled on the *padang*, the large green field in front of the old Moorish-type building that housed the government secretariat. On the other side of the field was the Selangor Club, one of the last outposts of colonial attitudes. There, crusty old Britishers still frowned on brash young Malayans who presumed to be their equals.

The air was filled with tense excitement as the people waited for midnight. With two minutes to go, all lights were switched off. A throbbing silence fell upon the throng packing the field and all roads leading to it. Then as the Secretariat clock – Malaya's Big Ben – struck 12 midnight, chiming the end of over eighty years of British rule, the lights came on again. To the solemn strains of God Save the Queen, the British flag was lowered. In its place rose the new Malayan flag and the new Malayan anthem *Negara-ku* or *My Country* – filled the night. People went wild with joy. Some shouted wordless outpourings of happiness. Others wept in jubilation. Above it all were thunderous roars of *Merdeka*! It rained for several hours afterwards, a clean, refreshing downpour. Most Malayans regarded this a good omen, taking the rain for heaven's blessing on a new nation.

The Selangor Club, Kuala Lumpur, today.

The actual handing over of power took place the following morning in the impressive Merdeka Stadium which had been completed just in time for the occasion. The attendance here was not as large as the Tunku had hoped for, but it was adequate for the purpose. With him on the special red-carpeted dais were the Sultans or their representatives, all decked in the regal costumes of Malay royalty.

At nine o'clock sharp, the bugler sounded a fanfare for the arrival of the Duke of Gloucester, the Queen's uncle and her representative to the independence ceremony. Behind the duke came his ADC bearing the constitutional documents for the transfer of power. The Duke of Gloucester was a portly figure in a plumed hat. He wore the white uniform of a field marshal. Standing at the head of the dais, under a royal umbrella, he read the Queen's message to the people of Malaya. He then turned and handed over the instrument of transfer to the Tunku.

Roars of *Merdeka* filled the stadium once more as the Tunku proclaimed independence. ". . . as from the thirty-first day of August, nineteen hundred and fifty-seven, the Federation of Malaya . . . is and with God's blessing shall be forever a sovereign democratic and independent state founded upon the principles of liberty and justice . . ." From the hills beyond, a 101-gun salute boomed out.

The Tunku felt a great sense of pride. On August 11, 1786, a Sultan of Kedah had given away the island of Penang to the British. Destiny had chosen a prince of the Royal House of Kedah to restore freedom not only to Penang but to the whole of Malaya on August 31, 1957. That was to become for him – and also, he believed, for the people of Malaya – a sacred day.

The Tunku recalled that in the years leading up to *Merdeka* he had been looked upon as something of a fractious man not only by the British but also by many Malayan politicians. These leaders, like Dato Onn bin Jaafar, were distinguished men who had made a mark in their own fields and had been specially chosen by the British for high posts in the administration. From their elevated positions they believed they had the widest possible perspective on the problems and prospects facing Malaya. They, too, wanted independence, but not so soon. They were convinced that Malaya's three million Malays and two-and-a-half million Chinese had not yet learned to live together and would be at each other's throats if Britain pulled out too quickly. There had to be sufficient time, at least ten years, to resolve this problem.

The same British-chosen men were highly alarmed at the Tunku's impatience. They regarded him as an irresponsible politician of the worst type. He had unquestionably been an irresponsible student in Britain, up to all kinds of mischief. He had taken twenty-one years to pass his law examinations in London and then had done poorly as a lawyer. Now he was in politics and playing it dangerously to get into the headlines.

In spite of British opposition, the Tunku met the CPM leadership in Baling. Then, manipulating the indecisive results of the Baling talks as his chief bargaining instrument against the British in London, won independence for Malaya. His fatherly approach belied a cunning intelligence. It took him ages to react but his reactions had a definite stamp of authority. He inspired a solid association between UMNO, the Malayan Chinese Association (MCA) and Malayan Indian Congress (MIC) under the benevolent umbrella of the Alliance Party. Even his detractors were beginning to be impressed by his quiet dominance of the Malayan political scene. For a reluctant politician, the lawyer/prince from Kedah wasn't doing too badly. The creation of the alliance with the Chinese and the Indians was a stroke of pure genius. And outwitting the communists in Baling wasn't pure luck either.

Those who later attempted to smash the alliance the Tunku had soldered failed to appreciate the human element that went into its making. Trust had been surrendered to the Tunku. Chinese and Indian politicians had placed their chips in his hands. They could have given them to Dato Onn bin Jaffar, who was the seasoned politician, in fact, the man who had formed UMNO in the first place. That wasn't lost on the Tunku. In his memory bank, apart from the 'slight file', he also maintained a compartment for grudges. Bigger still was the memory chest he maintained for recollections of genuine trust and friendship. As he liked saying: "We are not here only for politics." He considered himself lucky to have believed that all his life.

In the first municipal election in Kuala Lumpur in 1952, a small experiment was tried out which was to have a most profound impact on the future of Malaya. The Kuala Lumpur branches of UMNO and the MCA, erstwhile rivals, agreed to a form of political bonding to fight the election on a common platform. Their strategy was incredibly simple. UMNO would appeal to the Malays and MCA to the Chinese to vote for Alliance candidates. Observers were amazed at this political development.

UMNO existed to defend the position of the Malays. It claimed they were the natives of Malaya, with special rights, and these had to be defended against the encroachments of aliens, especially the Chinese. Strong suspicions were still smouldering among the Malay population. The CPM was predominantly Chinese and the Malays were led to believe by British propaganda that the CPM not only drew support from local Chinese communities but inspiration from Moscow, then from Peking.

The Malays also resented the economic strength of the Chinese. In every part of Malaya, the Chinese owned the businesses and banks, the shops and market stalls, the mills and factories, the buses and lorries. Little could be bought or sold except through the Chinese. In really big business, the British were probably still ahead, but before long most of them would be gone and the Malays feared that the Chinese would then take over the British interests as well. It was all simplistic but people then thought in terms of black and white. The colonials saw to that.

The MCA existed to protect the interests of the Chinese. Its primary aim was to win for them a proper place in their country of adoption. It was true their antecedents had come as aliens, but over the years no-one had worked harder than the Chinese to build Malaya and make it into what it had become. Pockets of the Chinese population may still nurse some affection for China, but these were now little more than vague stirrings in the blood. Most of these men were born in Malaya. Malaya was their home. It was true that they had won, through hard work, a big place in the economy, but they also wanted security and equality that could only come with equal political rights.

Between the Malays and the Chinese had always stood British colonial power, holding them apart. Backed by the might of the British Empire, it had once seemed a very superior and invincible power. But the Pacific war had changed all that.

To old hands, the experts, the 1952 Alliance experiment in Kuala Lumpur seemed a cruel joke. It was building false hopes. It was only a marriage of convenience and would never work. In a few weeks it would fall to pieces and this would give rise to new animosities.

But the experiment proved a tremendous success, and the Alliance pattern was rapidly extended throughout the country with sensational election triumphs. The MIC, sensing bright prospects ahead for Indians within the Alliance, quickly became the third partner. In the first general election in 1955 the Alliance captured 51 of the 52 seats. The British were still in power but they granted local autonomy to an Alliance government, and this proved a major step towards full independence.

As the Alliance went from victory to victory, its leaders watched the sad decline of one of the most outstanding political figures of the day. Dato Onn bin Jaafar who had emerged in 1946 to lead the Malays in a moment of crisis, forming UMNO, but then leaving it to create a new party, the Independence of Malaya Party (IMP), was pushed into the political wilderness.

Immediately after the last war the British had tried to change the entire political structure of Malaya. They wanted to merge the Malaya states, which were protectorates, into a single 'Malayan Union' making it a colony. The non-Malays welcomed it for it opened the door to political equality. The Malays, on the other hand, opposed it vehemently as a grave threat to their privileged position and decided to fight it.

The British made the mistake of sending a haughty representative, Sir Harold MacMichael, who breezed through the various sultanates, delivering each an ultimatum. The disrespect to the sultans made it easier for Dato Onn to rally the Malays under the banner of UMNO. The British were astonished at the unity they could never have predicted, indeed, never even have imagined. The Malayan Union was scrapped in 1948 and in its place came another constitution. This reinforced the special position of the Malays.

Dato Onn became a giant among his people. The Malays hero-worshipped him and many felt a stirring of memories of ancient legendary heroes who had once helped to build a glorious Malay Empire. Here at last was a man who could lead their race out of the disgrace of colonial domination. But Dato Onn's restless mind was already thrusting out in other directions. Despite his astuteness in forming UMNO, he was still under the spell of the British. It was the British who convinced him they would grant independence to Malaya only when the people of all races could live together harmoniously as one nation. It was the British who made him believe he could lead the way to winning independence. Of course, the time-frame had to suit them.

In 1951, Dato Onn asked UMNO to open its doors to non-Malays, but powerful sections of the party were not prepared to do this. Disappointed, he resigned from the party in August that year to form a new multi-racial grouping. It was a sorrowful occasion for UMNO, and marked the end of Dato Onn's career as Malaya's most important political leader. The crown went to a member of the Royal House of Kedah, Tunku Abdul Rahman, a little known figure at the time.

Dato Onn's IMP never had a chance. The Malays stayed with UMNO and the Chinese preferred to stick it out with the MCA. In the various elections that followed, the IMP was crushed by the Alliance and gradually faded away. Several years later Dato Onn died a bitter and broken man. A road leading to the Prime Minister's official residence in Kuala Lumpur was named after him.

The tragedy of Dato Onn left a deep impression on Malayan politics. The leaders of UMNO and the MCA took it as a warning that the people were not ready for multi-racial political parties. Their racial instincts were still too strong. It would take eons for a subtle balancing act to achieve an acceptable political power base and structure. For the present, though, the Alliance concept appeared to be the answer. Racial parties would continue their own separate existence but their leaders would get together in a loose organisation to sort out their mutual problems.

As a result of the Alliance, the years following independence were very happy ones. In spite of being a multi-racial society, there was more peace, harmony and progress in Malaya than in many other new countries that had no differences of race, language and religion. The economy expanded beyond everyone's expectations. Business was booming. New schools, hospitals and factories were springing up everywhere and new roads were being built at the rate of a mile a day.

The prophets of doom had withdrawn to the background, hoping to escape unnoticed.

RED RIBBONS ON A
SILVER PLATTER

When the plan for Malaysia began taking shape in late 1962, the Tunku set his heart on proclaiming the birth of the new nation on his lucky day – August 31, 1963. At the London conference on Malaysia, the date was agreed upon and fixed.

It was not to be.

President Sukarno of Indonesia, egged on by the Indonesian Communist Party (PKI) was persevering with his anti-Malaysia campaign. He insisted on being consulted or else there would be war. In 1963, the Tunku agreed to meet Sukarno in Manila in the first week of August. There, the Alliance leader was forced to consent to a United Nations mission to survey public opinion on merger among the people in the North Borneo states. The UN team was clearly unable to finish their appointed task by the end of August. There was therefore no choice but to postpone Malaysia Day beyond August 31. This was a severe blow to the Tunku's pride. He hated having to bow to the dictates of a man like Sukarno who had no business interfering with Malaysia.

Much has been made about the Tunku's penchant for certain dates and numbers. As a betting man, of course, he liked the thought of luck. It added colour to the drabness of unavoidable daily toil; it lifted one's spirit as essential routines ground on. What was wrong, for instance, in believing Saturday was your lucky day? Didn't it help make the trials of Friday less formidable?

The Tunku was always one for making life less burdensome. So we have to make important decisions; wouldn't a leisurely walk and some fresh air help clear our minds? Wouldn't an easy chat about small things make us more amenable to each other's bigger views? However, this frequently whimsical approach concealed to the uninitiated a truly sober side to the man. The Tunku observed certain priorities. The agreement he gave Sukarno in Manila was met and the August 31, 1963, proclamation of Malaysia was delayed. The Tunku was disappointed, but only briefly. A short postponement would preserve peace in the region; it was worth the price. National interest above personal whim.

The Tunku soon discovered Lee Kuan Yew had different ideas on this. Lee had not been invited by President Diosdado Macapagal of the Philippines to the August 6 Manila talks and therefore felt he was not bound by any agreement reached at that meeting. Furthermore, he was firmly opposed to giving any concessions to bullies like Sukarno. "This is the time for Malaysia to stand up and fight," Lee told the Australian Broadcasting Commission. "Do you think we should give in to an international blackmailer? We will not be gobbled up or knocked around like a football just because we happen to be the small guy in the region."

One wonders what the Tunku would have done – or what ruckus the UMNO leadership would have caused – had they all been privy to Lee Kuan Yew's other reason for pushing for an August 31 declaration of independence for Singapore. The Singapore leader had calculated he would announce general elections immediately after the originally proposed August 31 festivities.

Lee's firm stand against Sukarno was taken up by the leaders of Sabah and Sarawak. It put the Tunku in an embarrassing spot for he had already committed himself to the new arrangements reached in Manila. He asked the three leaders to consider his position. "I have gone a long way to make peace," he appealed to them. "I have humbled myself for the nation. Having done so to get Malaysia, it is wrong for anyone on our side to want to bring about a showdown."

The Tunku felt a softening of the attitudes of the representatives from Sabah and Sarawak but he failed to impress the Singapore leader. The situation worsened when Lee made a special trip to meet the men in Jesselton. After he left, the attitudes of the North Borneo politicians appeared to harden again. The Tunku was definitely displeased.

At a rally on August 31, 1963, brushing aside the misgivings of the Tunku, Lee Kuan Yew stood on the steps of City Hall and proclaimed the independence of Singapore as a prelude to joining Malaysia. He explained this was done not to oppose Malaysia but to consolidate it.

The development caused a stir in Kuala Lumpur where the Cabinet held an emergency meeting to consider its implications. It decided to ask the British government, which was still responsible for Singapore, to clarify the situation. The Commonwealth Relations Secretary, Duncan Sandys, who was in Kuala Lumpur at the time, provided a tactful explanation. He said independence for Singapore would require an Order-in-Council by the Queen. No such order had been made. Acting on this assurance the Tunku's government told Lee that his action had no legal or constitutional basis and asked him to rectify his stand.

Singapore's reaction came like a bombshell. Addressing a public rally, Lee made a fiery speech loaded with sarcasm. "You the people gave me the right to proclaim independence and I would like to see who says 'no'." He went on: "One of the sad things of Malaysia is the naïve approach of some people to whom power was handed over on a silver platter with red ribbons by British royalty in uniform."

Lee added: "Great men like George Washington and Lenin did not make their nations great by getting power in a ceremonial obeisance. Nearer home, when President Sukarno declared the independence of Indonesia, he was being sought by the Dutch army and was subsequently arrested. Perhaps for that reason he is less sympathetic to these genteel procedures for independence."

More than just noncompliant, dissenting language, Lee's speech struck the Tunku as a propaganda gift to Sukarno. He also found it particularly infuriating because it gave a number of more outspoken UMNO leaders further cause for consternation. They immediately accused Lee of sneering at them and called on the Tunku to review the whole question of Malaysia.

But the Tunku had given his word. Malaysia's inauguration would be celebrated in Singapore on September 16, 1963, and in Kuala Lumpur the following day. September 16 that year happened to be Lee Kuan Yew's 40th birthday. Whether the Tunku was aware of this coincidence or not has never been documented. Anyway, there had been decidedly more pressing things on the Malaysian leader's mind and he was beginning to feel stretched by the confrontation with Indonesia. The Philippines and Indonesia had withdrawn their ambassadors from Kuala Lumpur. Roars of *Ganyang Malaysia* – Crush Malaysia – had rung in the streets of Jakarta which were packed with rent-a-crowd demonstrators and agitators. Protesters had stormed and sacked the British and Malaysian embassies in the Indonesian capital. In Kuala Lumpur, not to be outdone, the locals had attacked the Indonesian Embassy.

Understandably, the Tunku approached Malaysian Inauguration Day in Kuala Lumpur with much trepidation. He was not alone. The British were just as worried and the fact of their unease could not be totally camouflaged by their ceremonial uniforms. Malaya and Britain had both witnessed and borne the brunt of an armed struggle at close quarters. The wounds of the Malayan Emergency had not exactly healed. Was the Tunku scared of Sukarno? Probably yes; but only a man as close to his race as the Tunku could tell.

One had to be an outsider without first-hand knowledge of the tribulations the peninsula had been through during the Emergency years to trust fully British resolve in the face of Sukarno's threats. The Tunku was convinced the British were finished fighting for the interests of their non-existent empire. The war against the CPM had passed for a colonial one and, in the event of a full-on confrontation with Indonesia, it would be easy for the United Kingdom to volunteer token aid. The danger was that eventually she would say Malaysia had, as an independent entity, the ultimate responsibility to defend its own sovereign rights.

That was how it stood for the Tunku in early September 1963.

The setting was more buoyant in Singapore.

For more than six months there had been coffee shop talk of an impending Singapore election. But it remained just that:

rumours. The opposition parties had grown extremely nervous. They could discover nothing from Lee's government. Every inquiry had been dismissed with a mysterious smile or cold, stubborn silence.

The election was sprung on them with startling suddenness. On the third of September 1963, three days after Lee's appearance on the City Hall steps declaring independence, Singapore called a general election. Nomination day: Sept 12. Polling Day remained a secret. Six hours after nominations closed, Radio Singapore put an end to the mystery. Polling Day would be September 21, providing a nine-day campaign period, the barest minimum allowed by the law. Lee's explanation: "A finality on this matter as soon as possible will make for peace and stability."

It was a cunning move by Lee; a master-stroke. The timing was perfect.

A feel-good mood wrapped the island. Singapore, soon to be the 14th state in the Malaysian Federation, was awash with expectation. There was so much to look forward to! People cheered Lee Kuan Yew. He had worked so hard for Malaysia's birth. How could he lose an election?

The shock tactics set off a blast of anger and disgust. Lee's opponents called him a bulldozer. "He wants a snap election – blitzkrieg style," said one of them. A former chief minister of Singapore, David Marshall, started immediate action in the courts to challenge the legality of Lee's moves. He lost. In Kuala Lumpur a disapproving Tunku followed the events.

From the start of the election campaign the Tunku began to notice a disquieting trend. His Alliance party in Singapore was fighting manfully with an air of confidence. He thought it had a good case to put to the voters. If they chose the Alliance they would have a government which would be on excellent terms with Kuala Lumpur. All the friction between the island and Malaya would disappear, the problems between them would melt away and Singapore would really become the 'New York' of Malaysia.

Lee's reply was filled with scorn. "Puppets!" he shouted, pointing an accusing finger at the Singapore Alliance leaders. He accused them of being Kuala Lumpur's stooges with no mind or will of their own. A few weeks earlier he had sneered as the

September 16, 1963, and Singapore is awash with celebrations of the birth of Malaysia. The photograph above shows the island's lavishly illuminated City Hall that drew thousands of excited revellers to the *padang* opposite and the waterfront beyond.

Singapore Alliance leaders marched dutifully to the Tunku's office in Kuala Lumpur with a list of candidates for vetting. Lee said they were receiving their orders from Kuala Lumpur and this would be bad for Singapore.

The PAP leader claimed he could see many teething problems ahead between the central government and the new island state. He said Singapore would need a strong government of its own to face up to Kuala Lumpur. Lee promised the voters that his party would have "the guts to stand up to the central government" and prevent any poaching on state rights.

The Tunku was astonished and perplexed at Lee's attitude. After fighting so hard to bring Singapore into Malaysia, he now seemed to regard the central government of Malaysia as a foreign government to be treated with suspicion and resisted at every point. If Lee persisted in this attitude what future could there be for Malaysia?

Five days after Malaysia was born, Singapore voted for Lee's spirit of defiance against the central government. The PAP won 37 seats. Thirteen went to the *Barisan Socialis*, a new party started by some of Lee's former colleagues. The *Barisan* was supposed to be infested with communist-influenced leaders. The Singapore Alliance, which had put up 42 candidates, failed to win a single seat. Worse, no less than 31 of its contenders lost their deposits.

The PAP won 47 per cent of the votes, the Singapore Alliance less than eight per cent. And to think that only 24 hours earlier the Alliance leaders in Singapore had sent this final message to the voters: "The PAP is dead. Don't waste your votes on them."

One astounding feature was the total defeat of the Tunku's Malay candidates in areas where Malay voters were in the majority. *The Straits Times* underlined the importance of this in a front-page account. The most significant development – suspected but not confirmed for some time – was the radical swing of Malay votes in the island from UMNO to the PAP.

Lee Kuan Yew was understandably jubilant. His dynamism could ignite bonfires of enthusiasm and support beyond Singapore; his ideas could be realised in other parts of Malaysia. His optimism was not unfounded. In the mainland, voters had also shied away from Alliance candidates in the recent town council elections. Lee had reason to hope and to believe that the peninsula was ready to vote for the lightning-flash emblem of the PAP as Singapore had done.

In Kuala Lumpur, the Tunku was shocked. The whole scenario puzzled him. He could understand the defeat of the MCA when pitted against the popular PAP. But the Singapore UMNO was supposedly well-organised. It had always enjoyed the support of the Malays and there was plenty of inspiration from Malaya where the Alliance had a history of a fantastic winning streak. With UMNO providing a sturdy backbone, the Alliance had won 54 per cent of the votes in the local government elections throughout Malaya, and almost three times as many seats as the combined opposition.

The Singapore results had the usually easy-going Tunku worked up. What disease was it that had afflicted the Singapore Malays? There could be only one explanation for UMNO's humiliating defeat on the island. There must be traitors at work among the Malays there. Perhaps Indonesian agents had turned them against their leaders because they had refused to bow to Sukarno.

There was another development that troubled the Tunku. Deep within the ranks of his party he could hear the low, menacing growl of a wounded tiger. A vicious temper was rising. Angry men in UMNO had already decided that the marauder was not really Sukarno but Lee Kuan Yew. He must be stopped before he could make any further inroads into UMNO's preserves.

TO HELL WITH SUKARNO

Towards the end of 1963, two months after the Alliance Party debacle in the Singapore general election, Senu bin Abdul Rahman, Malaysia's Ambassador to West Germany and a former Secretary-General of UMNO, returned to Kuala Lumpur from Bonn. He was summoned home to take up the new post of Director of Election Affairs in the Alliance. Observers read this to mean only one thing: elections in Malaysia.

Smarting from the Singapore embarrassment, Senu went about his task with great vigour. Additional hand-picked men were recruited to help him. Forty-nine Japanese cars were bought to provide a special transportation network. An 'Operations Room' was set up in the Alliance HQ in Kuala Lumpur from where the campaign would be directed with military efficiency. Nothing was taken for granted to ensure an Alliance – and therefore an UMNO – victory. Special committees were set up in every state and district to lay the groundwork. A massive election machine was completed with uncharacteristic haste and it was soon operating with impressive smoothness.

A month of campaigning started on March 22, 1964.

The Alliance's election strategy was brilliant in its sheer simplicity. There was to be no long-winded manifesto promising in detail what the party would do. It would go to the people with one single, vital objective set before them like a beacon in a dark cloudy sky.

It was decided the election battle cry of the Alliance would be 'National Survival'. The enemy was Sukarno whose *konfrontasi* of Malaysia was now becoming a grave menace. In Jakarta, Sukarno

The controversial Indonesian Ambassador in Kuala Lumpur, Lt-General Gusti Pengeran Harto Djatikusomo (right), receives orders from his boss – Indonesian President Sukarno. This picture was taken in 1964.

was under strong pressure from the Indonesian Communist Party (PKI) to carry out his threat to "crush" Malaysia. A special military command had been set up for this purpose and several Indonesian army battalions stood poised on the borders of Sabah and Sarawak. Indonesian guerillas were, in fact, crossing these borders almost daily to murder, plunder and destroy. Innocent villagers were being killed and their homes razed to the ground. A large raiding party armed to the teeth had pounced on a small unit of Malay soldiers at prayer. Indonesian saboteurs had crept into Singapore and detonated bombs in public places. At sea, Indonesian gunboats were robbing and kidnapping Malaysian fishermen. Indonesian planes were straying into Malaysian airspace and mysterious airdrops were being made into the nation's heartland.

Even more dangerous than all these attacks was the enemy within. To the Tunku's mind, a mind strongly influenced by Special Branch reports and briefings, there were two separate but mutually hostile groups working for the same objective – the destruction of Malaysia.

Special Branch analysts had assured him one group consisted of local communists who saw in Sukarno's confrontation campaign a new opportunity to seize power and avenge their previous defeat in Malaya. Such convenient 'cold war' interpretations are, of course, now well discounted by the emerging historical record.

The fact remains, though, that the Tunku was convinced at this time by Special Branch assurances the CPM was working in collusion with the Indonesian Communist Party (PKI), frantically trying to prepare the ground for a new insurrection. Indonesian agents were undoubtedly recruiting young Malaysians to Indonesia for secret training in guerrilla warfare and then infiltrating them back to selected towns on the peninsula. Some of these recruits certainly were sympathizers with the CPM cause. A few were actually dedicated comrades who had become cut-off from the main party when the CPM withdrew north to southern Thailand in the late 1950s.

That these events resulted from some grand cross-border plan, devised by devilishly cunning communist plotters was as fanciful as the notion that those being recruited were all hard-core comrades. They were, in the main, young, disenchanted, out-of-work labourers primarily from rural towns. As militants, they were sold on Sukarno's assurance of an uprising in the making. What was more, they counted on his word that he would support their fight with both 'volunteers' and arms from Indonesia. That the Tunku was seriously misinformed on these matters must be blamed on the Special Branch.

By this time the extreme left-wing Socialist Front, undoubtedly influenced by a communist element within its membership, was taking a vigorous anti-Malaysian stand. Drawing its support mainly from urban Chinese workers, the Front blamed the Malaysian government for all the trouble with Indonesia. In its eyes, Sukarno was blameless and his aggression completely justified. The Socialist Front demanded the break-up of Malaysia, the withdrawal of all British forces and a new peace offer to Sukarno. The Tunku, prompted by the Special Branch, held the view that the machinations of the Socialist Front were being closely coordinated with the PKI and the Indonesian military's guerrilla infiltration efforts. It all tied up neatly for public consumption but bore little resemblance to reality. Such coordination by the three communist functions, even had it been tried, would have proved impossible given their separate states of operational readiness. The threat from infiltrated guerrillas was real enough. The point was, most of them were not communist guerrillas.

The second hostile group, as seen by the Tunku, was made up of Malay racists; and here the information the Malaysian leader was receiving came from far more reliable intelligence. These were men who regarded Sukarno as a great Malay warrior returned from an ancient past to lead the Malay race to fresh glory. They aped him and hung his picture in their homes. Sukarno claimed to be a mystic who could look into the future. In that future he professed to see a new Malay empire embracing states of Malaysia, the Philippines and Indonesia – led, of course, by Sukarno. He peddled the idea that a Greater Indonesia would make the Malay race a world power capable of defending itself against the encroachments of foreigners, especially the Chinese.

Sukarno's followers in Malaysia found their political refuge in the Pan-Malayan Islamic Party (PMIP). Islam was their platform, the Holy Koran their political and religious authority, the fear of hell their main instrument of persuasion. They preached the gospel of rabid racial intolerance. They warned that any Muslim who mixed with non-Muslims was an infidel, doomed to hell and all other Muslims should have nothing to do with him. They taught that UMNO, by entering into a partnership with Chinese and Indians, had become a party of infidels, and any Muslim who joined it or voted for it would incur the wrath of God. The PMIP distributed special talismans, made by a Chinese firm in Hongkong, bearing the inscription that the Prophet Mohammed was the leader of their party. They sold special love charms to Malay women, with a warning that the charms would not work if the women voted for infidels.

A sinister plot was followed. Malay youths, seized with a sudden religious fervour, were recruited into a conspiracy and sworn to secrecy. They took sacred oaths and, filled with righteousness, they left their villages to train in Jakarta from where they hoped to come back, crush Malaysia and help establish a Greater Indonesia.

In the remote Muslim areas of north-eastern Malaya, where the PMIP had its lairs, the party's strident teachings created utter confusion. Wives began to doubt if they were still properly married to their husbands who had become infidels by supporting UMNO. Some were afraid to attend the funerals of their fathers for similar reasons. Weddings were boycotted by brothers and sisters who were utterly confused but nevertheless decided to err on the side of caution.

The Socialist Front, with its left-wing Chinese following, and the PMIP with its racist Malay support, were now challenging the government of Tunku Abdul Rahman to prove its mandate. By what right had they chosen a course that was leading to full-scale conflict with Indonesia? Their challenge could not be ignored. These were parties with substantial followings. In the 1959 election, they had won 34 per cent of the vote.

The Tunku accepted the challenge confidently. His instincts told him that the situation contained all the ingredients for a great Alliance victory, and his instincts had hardly ever led him astray. He could sense a deep revulsion swelling up among a greater number of Malays against Sukarno's bullying arrogance. The attack on young Malay troops as they knelt in prayer in their jungle camp could never be forgiven. Furthermore, the rebellious Malays had begun realising that Sukarno was perhaps not capable of leading them to a better and brighter future after all. He might well drag them down to the level of Indonesia, to chaos and misery.

The Chinese, too, were watching in horror the terrible cruelty being inflicted on members of their race in Indonesia. Sukarno had closed, first their schools and then their newspapers. They were pushed out of much of the wholesale trade and this was followed by a decree banning them from retail trade in the rural areas. There, they were driven out without mercy and their shops and businesses seized. In the towns to which they fled, they found themselves the target of ferocious anti-Chinese riots in which their property was looted and destroyed. The Indonesian government then began to banish thousands of them to Communist China, a land they had never known.

The Tunku judged that conditions were perfect for his vote-winning battle cry – *National Survival*. He could now go to the people and warn them that a vote for the Socialist Front or the PMIP would be a vote for Sukarno, a vote for slavery and eventual doom.

On the other hand, a vote for the Alliance would be a vote for Malaysia, for freedom and continuing prosperity. He was sure the people would make only one choice. They would choose his party.

The Tunku decided that the contest should be confined to the states of Malaya, as the new states of Singapore, Sabah and Sarawak had just had their own elections. Their turn would come again in the first pan-Malaysian election planned for 1969.

He was in for another surprise. Singapore's PAP had set up a branch in Malaya and its sensational victory across the Causeway six months earlier had given it added confidence. It was no longer a small, parochial party which could be confined to its island base. It was now ready for the bigger national arena of Malaysia. Lee Kuan Yew announced that for the present his party would make only a token entry, with a limited number of candidates.

The Tunku was taken aback. In the difficult negotiations leading up to merger, Lee had given his word to stay out of this election. He repeated this promise during the elections in Singapore. Now he was breaking it. No one could deny Lee was firmly on the side of Malaysia, but the Tunku decided PAP participation in the 1964 contest would cause much ill will and complication.

The Tunku's fears were harshly confirmed when Lee explained the reasons why the PAP was veering from an agreed course. Lee seemed confident that UMNO could successfully resist attempts to weaken its hold on the Malays. It could take on and beat the PMIP. But Lee professed to see the MCA in a dangerous state of decline.

His diagnosis of the MCA's condition was quite alarming. Lee apparently believed that the MCA was rapidly losing support because its leaders were self-seeking men with little integrity. He regarded them as weak-kneed leaders who could not stand up to UMNO for non-Malay rights. To protect their own business interests, they were selling the non-Malays and especially the Chinese down the drain.

The discontent among the urban Chinese voters could result in a protest vote against the MCA. In this scenario, the Socialist Front would benefit. If this happened, Sukarno would infer that the anti-Malaysia forces were growing stronger and he would be greatly encouraged. At all costs, these protest votes had to be rescued from the Socialist Front.

To Lee, there was an obvious remedy. He had already proved in Singapore that he could pull in the sophisticated urban voters. The PAP would now rally the non-Malays in the urban areas of Malaya and save them from the Socialist Front, while UMNO could go ahead and consolidate its mass Malay base in the rural areas. UMNO and the PAP could then work together in a more realistic partnership in which non-Malay interests would be effectively represented.

The Tunku's deepest suspicions were immediately aroused. He had worked with the MCA for twelve years and over that period had been able to establish a vast reservoir of goodwill and trust with them. Together they had been able to solve many difficult and delicate problems. They had been through hard times and their loyalty to each other was beyond question. This partnership had been the basis of Malaysia's tremendous success.

Lee, the Tunku decided, was a totally different proposition. By now the Tunku regarded him as a brilliant, calculating machine who appeared to have no genuine appreciation for trust and loyalty among friends. The Tunku saw Lee as a man who kept a friend only as long as this was useful and then discarded him when the friendship no longer brought in results, or worse, had become a political liability. In Singapore he had used the communists in his climb to power, but once safely ensconced, he had them incarcerated. Undoubtedly this was good for Singapore but it also revealed Lee's character and methods. To the Tunku, Lee was a man who clearly lacked the warmth that made all the difference in human relations. The Tunku was now convinced Lee had yet to learn the value of generosity, to see why there was sometimes a need to offer something on trust or to give something in charity.

The Tunku remembered the lead up to Malaysia and how most days dealing with the Singapore politician proved nightmares. The fuss, the frenetic pace, the non-stop pleading to be heard and understood. The Tunku recalled finding it a strain to remain gracious in the presence of such stolid arrogance. It was beyond belief. The Tunku began recalling recent history. Lee had displayed the workings of his enormous ego in London, in declaring Singapore independence and during the Singapore election. He was now demonstrating it once more by suggesting he would provide the intellectual leadership that could satisfy the sophisticated urban voters of Malaysia. The Tunku listened and wondered. Did Lee regard the Alliance leaders as crude, backward men who were good enough only for the rural voters? Could the reports of some disgruntled UMNO leaders then be accurate – that Lee, in one of his speeches, had even referred to the Tunku as a man who lacked the calibre to be a national leader? The Alliance leader had dismissed this as mere anti-Lee talk within UMNO geared to making him more disaffected with the PAP's top man. Still, it had irked him. Now, he wondered. . .

The Tunku felt comfortable and safe in his association with the MCA which was led by Tan Siew Sin who had inherited its leadership from his father, Dato Sir Tan Cheng Lock who had sat with the Tunku at the Baling talks in 1955. It was an easy, friendly affair with the MCA. Everyone there readily accepted him as *Bapa Malaysia* – Father of Malaysia. The MCA had never challenged his leadership, just as it had never challenged the special, pre-eminent political position of the Malays. As a result, concessions were easily given and accepted on either side. The Alliance lived and thrived in a healthy spirit of compromise. The Malays felt secure behind their special rights and privileges while the Chinese were grateful for the opportunity to make a good living.

With Lee Kuan Yew, the Tunku began to see it would never be the same. Lee was a politician in a hurry to change things. The

Malay prince could not abide by such impatience. Lee would insist on readjusting the balance at once. He would want to draw a clear line between himself as leader of the non-Malays and the Tunku as leader of the Malays – two leaders meeting on equal terms. And then he would again bargain in his grim, unrelenting fashion, just as he had done in London. He would pay lip service to the special position of the Malays, the Tunku thought, but would set out to erode it. Lee would cause the racial lines between the Malays and the Chinese to harden; his combative fashion would lead to the evaporation of communal harmony. Whatever the Tunku and his allies had built could be smashed so easily and what assurance was there that a better arrangement would be achieved?

Never again, the Tunku would now and then remark, would he be pushed into affixing his signature on the back of an envelope, albeit one from the sitting room of a suite at the Ritz Hotel.

The Tunku was convinced that the Malays in the mainland would never trust Lee. They had already judged his character and his intentions. They regarded him as the spearhead of a dangerous Chinese attack on their special position, and they resented his entry into the Malaysian election. Some UMNO leaders were already saying that Lee should be fought not only with political weapons.

Two weeks after the PAP entered the election, the Tunku rejected Lee's campaign approach as 'glib talk'. He announced that the Alliance partners would swim or sink together. "Even if there are only five MCA members left, we will always stand together united in a common purpose," the Alliance leader declared. He praised the MCA for remaining steadfast to the principles of honesty and sincerity, a comment which was widely taken to mean that he had not found the same qualities in the PAP.

Lee was not easily deterred. He remained a persistent suitor, insisting that if he was not wanted today, he would have to be accepted tomorrow, together with his ideas for building a stronger Malaysia on non-communal lines. It was inevitable, he said. He had a bagful of subtle, ingenious arguments, but the harder he tried the more hostile he found the UMNO leadership.

The Tunku was supremely confident his Alliance would succeed, even without the help of the PAP. He was sure his party would ride to a great victory on his pledge to defend Malaysia. It was a pledge that the PAP would also be compelled to support, thereby helping the Alliance and getting nothing in return.

By its own admission, the PAP was making only a token appearance in the election. It was contesting only nine of the 104 seats at stake. It was merely flexing its muscles, testing out its strength for the next election in 1969. The Tunku felt sure the voters, realising the nation was in peril, would decide in favour of the Alliance Party. The situation demanded a strong, stable government which could stand up to Sukarno and only the Alliance could give them that.

In an early election statement, the PAP said: "Every ballot paper cast in favour of the Socialist Front is one more bullet for the Indonesian terrorists. The Socialist Front is the advance guard of the Indonesian Communist Party, just as the PMIP is the beach-head in Malaysia for Indonesian racialism." That became the main theme of the election with many variations provided by Alliance leaders.

The Tunku followed up: "You have one choice and one choice only – do you want to defend your democratic heritage or surrender it to Sukarno? Do you want to become a colony of Indonesia where people are asked to eat rats?"

Tun Abdul Razak, Deputy Prime Minister declared: "Subandrio (Indonesia's Foreign Minister) has said that in Indonesia the Chinese have been fixed so that they are no longer a danger to Indonesia. My Malaysian friends of Chinese origin, I hope you know what that means. Think carefully before you vote. A vote for the Socialist Front or the PMIP is a vote for Sukarno."

Senu bin Abdul Rahman, Director of Election Affairs attested: "I knew Sukarno personally for four and a half years and I can tell you he is power drunk. He is following the foot-steps of Hitler and Mussolini. The only way to stop him from taking Malaysia is to vote for the Alliance."

Mohammed Khir Johari, Minister for Agriculture pronounced: "We have not escaped from the British lion to fall into the waiting jaws of the Indonesian crocodile. But that will happen if you vote for the Socialist Front or the PMIP."

Tan Siew Sin, Minister of Finance volunteered: "An Indonesian takeover of this country would subject the Chinese to the most unspeakable horrors and agony. Yet there are Chinese who support a party which practically incites the Indonesians to take over this country."

Syed Jaafar Albar, Secretary-General of the UMNO mused: "A dragon is waiting across the sea to swallow us. That dragon is Sukarno and the Socialist Front and the PMIP want to lead him into our country".

Dato (Dr) Ismail bin Dato Abdul Rahman, Minister of Internal Security stated flatly: "The Chinese will be the first to lose their heads if Indonesia takes over this country. You will suffer the same fate as the Chinese in Indonesia. But Sukarno will not dare continue his confrontation if there is a landslide victory for the Alliance."

And it went on and on and on. Lee Kuan Yew provided an occasional diversion with provocative statements about non-racial politics and the dynamic economic policies of the PAP. UMNO listened to him with growing suspicion and hostility. To them, his socialism was a disguise concealing a stealthy attack on the special position of the Malays. His PAP was like poisonous mushrooms, popping out of rebellious soil. One day, the soil would have to be treated. In the meantime, all attention must be focused on Sukarno. His name alone was driving thousands of doubtful voters into the Alliance net.

The Tunku kept up a spirited performance which reached its climax at an election rally in the small town of Bagan Serai. Thousands greeted his arrival with roars of 'Merdeka!' He was suitably inspired and rose to the occasion. He recalled that in spite of Britain's overwhelming military power in the long struggle against the CPM, it was left to him to deliver the final knock-out blow. If Sukarno now dared to attack, he too would be knocked out in the same way.

Raising his voice and waving his fist in the air, the Tunku shouted: "Come Sukarno! Come Indonesia! Malaysia is ready if you want to fight. We have friends and we can fight you and crush you. No one except God himself can crush Malaysia." The crowd went wild with excitement and roared its approval.

The voters went to the polls on April 24 with a final message from the Tunku ringing in their ears: "You are Malaysians – vote for Malaysia." They gave him a stupendous victory. They gave the Alliance 89 seats out of 104. The Socialist Front limped home with two seats. The PMIP was hacked down from 13 to nine.

The biggest surprise was the PAP's humiliating defeat. The party won only one seat with a narrow margin, while three of its men actually lost their deposits. Obviously, the huge crowds which had listened to the man from Singapore with enthusiasm chose not to vote for him. Lee sent a generous message to the Tunku: "No one in the world can now doubt that you lead the people of Malaysia in their desire to build an independent and democratic nation, separate and distinct from Indonesia."

At his home the Tunku was jubilant over his extraordinary triumph. "This victory is a momentous one for our country and has given us much courage to face our enemies with absolute confidence," he said, adding: "To hell with Sukarno."

RIOTS FROM INDONESIA

The Tunku set out on an important mission on July 4, 1964. He flew to London to tell his Commonwealth opposite numbers that Sukarno's *konfrontasi* was getting out of hand. If they could get together and warn the Indonesian dictator to lay-off, it would be a great help to Malaysia.

He was disappointed. Some of the Commonwealth prime ministers were totally indifferent to Malaysia's plight. One even held the view that Malaysia was actually the aggressor. The Tunku would later recoil at the impertinence. Imagine it! Imagine tiny Malaysia with ten million people committing aggression against giant Indonesia with 100 million.

"Some of these people," said the Tunku, "feel it is not smart, not fashionable, to align themselves with the West even though they get money from the West. In Malaysia, we don't shilly-shally. We believe honesty counts – in our internal and external affairs." For the Tunku, it was a good thing Malaysia had such close and reliable friends in Britain, Australia and New Zealand.

After a fortnight in Britain, the Malaysian leader flew to the United States for talks with the Americans on the same subject. He felt the US could prove a key to the problem. President John Kennedy had greeted the birth of Malaysia with glowing words of welcome but since then the Americans had been playing a double game. They seemed to think that because Indonesia was ten times the size of Malaysia, she was ten times more important and deserved to be pampered. This misconception was being held at Malaysia's expense.

This candid photograph of Lt-General Djatikusomo taken in April, 1965, would suggest that the manipulative diplomat's joy at this time is directly proportional to the deteriorating relationship between Kuala Lumpur and neighbouring Singapore.

The Tunku believed it was therefore important to tell the American people what Malaysia was and what it stood for. In turn, they asked him what he considered to be Malaysia's greatest achievement. "I told them our people, comprising many races and religions, are happily living side by side. This is what I am proud of."

Words spoken too soon. An urgent telegram reached the Tunku in the town of Williamsburg, Virginia, two days after his speech on Malaysian harmony. Violent race riots had broken out in Singapore on July 21. He wept. He would remember it as one of the unhappiest days of his life. He wanted to fly home immediately but another cable arrived telling him the situation was under control.

How was he to explain this to the American people after what he had said to them earlier? The casual observer might now begin to believe Sukarno, buy his claim that Malaysia was an artificial creation which could not survive, that it would be torn apart by racial violence. The Americans might even feel it would be better to get rid of Malaysia at once before it caused more instability in Southeast Asia. The Tunku felt deeply troubled. Anyone who knew Malaysia well would know that this was untrue. Malays and Chinese had lived together for generations without such trouble. But how could he now say this to people who only trusted what they read in their daily papers?

More importantly, how had these dreadful riots come about? The Malaysian leader racked his brain till the wee hours and then a name he had read through various reports became distinctly clear: Gusti Pengeran Harto Djatikusomo, a Javanese general who was Indonesia's Ambassador to Malaysia until the outbreak of Confrontation.

When he was based in Kuala Lumpur, Djatikusomo used to walk through the streets on many an evening, dressed like a local, in sarong and slippers. He frequented the capital's Kampong Bahru area where he knocked on doors and spent hours telling the Malays they were being victimized and robbed by the Chinese. He told them the birth of Malaysia would mean the loss of their country. He spoke in quiet, conspiratorial tones, urging the Malays to drive the Chinese out of Malaysia. The Malays should join forces with Indonesia so that, with combined strength, they could destroy the others, meaning the Chinese.

Djatikusomo also went quietly, but often, to chat with the soldiers of the Malay Regiment stationed in Port Dickson. There he taunted them and asked why they still tolerated British officers. He demanded: "Why can't you have your own officers as we do in Indonesia?"

In Singapore, Djatikusomo's agents did their work as efficiently. The ground was fertile. In those early days, the Malays in Singapore felt neglected and marginalised. Although they lived in a city with bright lights and merry laughter, they led essentially a rural existence and were poor in the extreme. True enough, there were also impoverished Chinese. But the perception of a Chinese island state did not help the Malays' sense of isolation. They had believed that when Singapore joined Malaysia, they would come into their own and life would automatically improve. When this had not happened sooner than they had envisioned, the Malays became discontented and it was easy for provocateurs to goad them into violence.

The Tunku returned home from his overseas trip on August 14 to a touching welcome. Everywhere he went people greeted him as children would a father after a long absence. They seemed to feel safer with him around. One of the first things he did was to visit Singapore. "Our beloved Singapore," he called it. He toured the riot-stricken areas and felt the agony of those terrible days. This resulted in an inspired speech one night to a large mixed gathering of Malays and Chinese. It was filled with compassion and a gentle humour, the kind of humour that encourages men to laugh in spite of their pain.

He reminded them of Djatikusomo, and Sukarno's plans to crush Malaysia either through open aggression or by inciting internal racial strife. He had tried to make peace with Sukarno, he told them, but it was impossible to deal with such a man. He was a man without a conscience or a soul.

"He asked me to go to Tokyo and I went to Tokyo. He asked me to go to Manila and I went to Manila. Then he asked me to go once more to Tokyo and I went to Tokyo again. But he went there to enjoy himself. Every day he changed his uniform! Sometimes he wore white, sometimes he wore black, sometimes blue, sometimes khaki. I thought to myself: What is this? Here we are discussing vital issues involving nations, and there he is changing his uniforms!"

The Tunku went on to explain how he had swallowed his pride and put up with Sukarno's nonsense for the sake of Malaysia. It would be such a great country. There was enough room in Malaysia for all, enough natural resources and opportunities for everyone to live happily without quarrelling, fighting and killing.

The trouble was that some Malays were highly strung, the Tunku told his audience. Poke one of them in the back and say 'wolf' and he'd jump and repeat 'wolf, wolf, wolf, wolf.' But from now on, the Tunku admonished, they must learn to control themselves. He promised the Malays in Singapore that he would look into their problems and try to brighten their lives. He informed them the Singapore government was also keen to address this matter. Now that conditions were going to improve there should be no more complaints and no more listening to trouble-makers.

The Tunku's presence in Singapore was like a healing balm. Othman Wok, Singapore's Minister of Welfare, said it had done a great deal to boost the morale of the people. They now felt reassured. Even Lee Kuan Yew publicly admitted that only the Tunku could heal Singapore's wounds, "in his own time and in his own way". He added that he had full faith in the Tunku.

But Lee was saying a lot of other things as well. It was becoming clear now to the Malaysian prime minister that life with Lee would be a complex and trying affair, one full of unpleasant surprises. If Lee had a theory, no one could bottle it up. The harder anyone tried, the louder he would shout. It was obvious now that he had his own views on the riots.

Lee agreed with the Tunku that the Indonesians had a big hand in the trouble. But he was also convinced that other men in Kuala Lumpur were equally to blame: racial fanatics from the Tunku's own party! These men, angry at UMNO's defeat in Singapore, had rushed down to the island to apply their own remedy. Their method was to try to win back support for their party by causing trouble.

The Tunku would recall Lee saying that UMNO leaders came to Singapore and started shouting: 'Malays unite! The Chinese are oppressing you. They are chasing you out from the city." This, according to Lee, had created a situation the Indonesian agents were able to exploit.

It was obvious to the Tunku that the man Lee was gunning for was Syed Jaafar Albar, the then UMNO Secretary General. Lee and Albar had never hit it off from the start and had become deadly enemies. Lee was now demanding a Commission of Inquiry into the riots in the hope that it would fix the blame on 'Albar and his merry men'. The Tunku advised Lee against pushing too hard for this. They could hold a quiet post-mortem, but raking up the smouldering embers in a full-scale public inquiry could be highly dangerous. The Tunku was sure an immediate answer to Lee's demand would only worsen the prevailing ugly animosities. It would be much wiser to wait till feelings had subsided.

On September 2, six weeks after the first riots, Singapore blew up again. This time there was no mistaking the finger on the trigger. It was clearly Indonesian. The trouble began just as a force of Indonesian paratroopers were being airdropped into the Malayan jungle about a hundred miles to the north.

In Singapore that night, a trishaw man in his late thirties was desperately tired after a long, hard day of pedalling for a few dollars to feed his family. Life was tough but he took it in his stride and was known to all as a friendly, affable person. He pulled to the side of a road and was soon asleep. Out of the shadows a group of men pounced on him, stabbing and slashing savagely.

A few hours later, a 54-year-old woman, returning from the market, was set upon by a group of killers. For a moment she stood petrified as iron rods and wooden poles came crashing down upon her, and then she sank to the ground broken and bleeding. She later died in hospital.

The Tunku was shaken. Everything had seemed to be going along so nicely! The people of Singapore had returned to work as usual. Plans were being finalised to give the Malays a better deal as he had promised. Why, then, had riots broken out again? It was his view that thugs and gangsters hired by Sukarno's agents were responsible for these brutal killings, carried out in a manner designed to arouse passions on all sides. Once again the hotheads took to the streets, leaving a toll of 13 dead and nearly a hundred injured.

He decided to get to the bottom of it all.

The investigations showed that there were traitors within the country actively working for Sukarno. These men had gone among the Malays in Singapore telling them to ignore the Tunku's assurances, urging that now was the time to go for revenge against the Chinese or their future would be doomed. Children of 12 and 13 were paid to throw stones, women on their way to market were asked to spread hair-raising stories. The aim behind these tactics was obvious. If people continued to stir up racial trouble, there would be no need for Sukarno to send his guerrillas to Malaysia. Malaysia would destroy itself.

Once again the Tunku spoke to the Malays, assuring them there was nothing to fear. Their political position was unassailable and their rights were enshrined in the Constitution. At the same time they must respect the rights of others. He counselled: "Our strength must be used not to destroy but to build up this country into a home for ourselves and our children."

A few days after this speech, the Tunku struck back at the enemy. Possible ringleaders and hundreds of thugs and gangsters supposedly employed by them were arrested. A state of emergency was declared throughout the country. Singapore gradually began to simmer down.

Dato Syed Jaafar Albar, UMNO's Secretary General
when this photograph was taken in May, 1965,
greatly enjoyed his supporters' acknowledgement
of his role as Enemy No 1 to Singapore leader
Lee Kuan Yew.

STAB IN THE BACK

Those in Peninsular Malaysia who knew and cared for Singapore – many families, Chinese, Malay, Indian and Eurasian, had relatives on either side of the Causeway – sensed that something had gone terribly wrong on the island. It used to be a cheerful city but in recent years the happiness appeared to have gone out of its life. It had taken to wearing a chip on its shoulder and a scowl on its face. In the rush to prove itself, a pugnacious mood prevailed. It was a city that seemed forever spoiling for a fight.

No one could deny that Sukarno had been behind the July riots and, clearly, local people had helped as well. They had created the atmosphere of unmitigated tension that had to explode in some way. Lee Kuan Yew had directly accused Albar of inciting the Malays. But what about the September riots? Albar was in hospital when these began. What happened then?

The truth, the Tunku finally claimed to his confidants, was that Lee himself was partly to blame. He and his colleagues had turned Singapore not merely into a 'hot-bed' but a 'red-hot bed' of politics. By constantly harping on racial issues they had prepared the ground for Sukarno. Singapore was obviously suffering from the wrong type of government! The Tunku reflected on this for a few days and decided to share his thoughts with the people of Singapore. On September 20, 1964, he flew down to the island city to speak to the leaders of the Singapore Alliance. "There is an under-current to contest my leadership of the Malaysian people by trying to make out that I am a leader of the Malays only," he told them.

The Tunku's meaning was absolutely clear. The person trying to challenge his leadership was Lee Kuan Yew, the man he felt he had saved from political extinction by allowing Singapore to join Malaysia. Now Lee was hoping to oust him and become Prime Minister of Malaysia on the votes of the non-Malays. What a stab in the back!

He advised the Singapore Alliance leaders to work harder to defeat Lee. The people of Singapore, he said, wanted the Alliance to lead them to greater unity with the rest of Malaysia. "They are fed up with all these giddy and stupid politics which do not take into account the happiness, wellbeing and harmony of the people."

Giddy politics! There was much more of it in the following weeks, in spite of the growing threat from Indonesia. Indonesian troops were violating the Malaysian frontier every day. Sukarno's guerrillas were operating deep within Malaysian territory and his gunboats were constantly harassing Malaysian fishermen. As a result the defence bill had risen from $1 million to nearly $2 million a day.

The Tunku was determined to defend Malaysia. Sukarno was claiming the right to crush a small country simply because he didn't like its politics. If Sukarno got away with it, no other small country would be safe. Therefore, every cent that it cost to resist him would be money well spent. History would remember this as a glorious feat.

New taxes were introduced in November, 1964, to raise the additional money needed for defence. Some opposition was inevitable, but the attitude of Lee and his colleagues in Singapore shocked the Tunku. The Singaporeans mounted a massive campaign against the new taxes. They used them to try to discredit the central government and divide the people. The Tunku found it intolerable.

On December 9, 1964, the Tunku went back to Singapore to deliver a warning. He spoke of his dream to make Singapore the 'New York' of Malaysia. It was a grand city, the pride of Malaysia. In nearly every way it was better than Hongkong. But Singapore's weakness was its politics. "There are so many types of politicians in Singapore. There are those who are red hot," the Tunku stated. "There are those of soft pink. There are those with a yellow and brown-tinged chauvinistic tendency. There are greenish banner-waving ones and there are lightning-flash ones." The lightning-flash was, of course, the PAP symbol.

The Tunku then warned these politicians 'of various colours and tinges and flashes' that if they continued to disagree with him the only solution would be for Singapore to break away from Malaysia. What a calamity that would be for Singapore and Malaysia!

On January 31, 1965, the moon brought the Chinese and Malays together in joint celebrations. It was Chinese New Year, the year of the serpent. Some would condemn the serpent for its venom and hideousness. Others would praise it for its grace and beauty and its supernatural powers. Whatever their views on the serpent, the Chinese celebrated their new year with vast quantities of birds' nests, sharks' fins, roast suckling pigs, stewed ducks and thousands of bottles of brandy and whisky. They filled the days and nights with the din of fire-crackers.

The Chinese New Year, fixed according to the lunar calendar, coincided with the new moon for which the Malays had been waiting. It marked the end of the Muslim fasting month of Ramadan and the start of Hari Raya celebrations. Malay households decorated the land with millions of little oil lamps. Necklaces of multi-coloured, tiny lights hung around their homes where tables were laden with special dishes and cakes. In their new clothes they did their *balik kampung* (homecoming). Families and friends were reunited.

It was a good omen, this coming together of two great festivals. The Tunku decided to mark the occasion with a joint message to the Malays and the Chinese. He tried to sound hopeful but it was clear that his thoughts were still on the politicians in Singapore, particularly Lee Kuan Yew. They were talking of strife and strain and trouble and bloodshed ahead. Wherever they went they fashioned gloom in the minds of the people.

The Tunku was dismayed by newspaper headlines that greeted him nearly every other day.

"KUAN YEW WARNS OF FURTHER STRESSES AND STRAINS"
"PROGRESS OR DESTRUCTION? WHICH PATH, ASKS LEE"
"LEE WARNS: WE CAN LOSE OUR PROSPERITY"

"In this hour of trial and tribulation," said the Tunku, "such talk is indeed foolish and harmful and dangerous, and I say shame on them. We have to think of service to this country, and unity should be the keynote of our discussions."

Midway through the week-long Chinese New Year and Hari Raya celebrations, the Tunku's attention was called to an astonishing report published in the *Washington Post* under the headline: "Singapore Chief asks US help on race accord."

The Tunku was astounded but decided to withhold comment. He left it to Albar to reply and Albar hit back with his usual vigour. He attacked Lee for inviting a foreign power to meddle in Malaysia's internal affairs. Albar also attacked foreign press correspondents for denigrating Malaysia's leaders.

One month later, Lee Kuan Yew took off on a month-long tour of Australia and New Zealand at the invitation of their governments. He claimed he wanted to show them Malaysia was really worth defending. He did that very well, but, as his opponents in UMNO would say, he also did a lot more besides! They would soon be asserting that Lee's main aim was to project not Malaysia but Lee Kuan Yew. The average Australian listening to him could be forgiven for thinking that Lee was the prime minister, the foreign minister and the only politician of merit in the whole of Malaysia.

The Australians were won over by Lee's hard-hitting eloquence. Wherever he spoke, hundreds of enthusiastic students turned up to listen to him. The Australian press praised him lavishly and lapped up everything he said. Not satisfied with attacking Indonesia, Lee began to snipe at the central government in Malaysia. He took aim at the Malay 'Ultras'. This was the epithet he had chosen for prominent UMNO leaders he regarded as racial extremists. "Who are the Ultras?" asked Lee. He provided the answer: "They have been identified as Malay extremists who are trying to appeal to the Malays by fabricating myths so as to incense them into irresponsible action. They are the real enemies of a multi-racial Malaysia which cuts across race, religion and language."

But worse, as far as the Tunku was concerned, was Lee's reference to the racial percentages in Malaysia. Malays – 39 per cent, non-Malays – 61 per cent. Surely, the Tunku fretted, the man must know that nothing would alarm the Malays more than to be reminded in this fashion that they had become a minority in their own land. This was playing right into the hands of the real extremists. They were not Lee's 'Ultras' but other men who regarded the Indonesians as their blood-brothers and had always felt that the Malays should join up with the Indonesians to 'fix' the

Chinese. If Lee wasn't careful, he would frighten the Malays into supporting these men, and they would ruin the future not only for himself but for all Chinese in Malaysia.

Still, to UMNO and the Tunku, Lee was evidently thinking of other things. Having appealed to the United States to interfere in Malaysia's internal affairs, he was now inviting Australia and New Zealand to do the same. The Tunku watched and listened in silence and his hatchet men were battle-ready. Khir Johari protested angrily that Lee had made the central government look a "bunch of the worst fellows in the world". In Kuala Lumpur certain attitudes were beginning to harden dangerously.

Malaya's Prime Minister Tunku Abdul Rahman and Indonesia's President Sukarno meet in Japan in June, 1963, in a vain attempt to resolve mounting friction over the projected formation of Malaysia – a proposal Sukarno had dismissed as nothing more than a British neo-colonialist plot.

A NEW STORM

On May 1, 1965, Tunku Abdul Rahman was in Tokyo after spending four pleasant days in South Korea. The official reason for his visit to Japan was the Asian Youth Soccer Tournament. He was President of the Asian Football Confederation. The Malaysian PM was a great believer in sport and nothing could perk up his spirit more than an exciting game of soccer. He strongly believed that sport could build character, broaden the mind, create a sense of team spirit and develop loyalty. He was also convinced that it could promote friendship between man and man, nation and nation.

There were two other reasons for the Tunku's visit to Japan. His eyes had been tearing for some time and he wanted to consult a Japanese specialist. But more important, he was hoping Sukarno would come to Japan for peace talks. Not that he enjoyed talking to Sukarno, although the Indonesian leader could produce rich verbal spice on such matters as love and sex. Sukarno was mad, a destructive chap, totally unpredictable, but for the sake of peace the Tunku would forget his pride and wait for Sukarno if necessary. For days Sukarno had kept the world, and the Tunku, guessing. He was having fun in Jakarta, changing his mind every other day about going to Tokyo. Finally he announced his decision. On May Day he went before a massive rally in Jakarta and sang: "Who says I want to go to Tokyo. I am happier to stay with my people..." The crowds clapped, cheered wildly and sang along with him.

The Tunku was not greatly disappointed for he had been prepared for this. "I have become hardened to Sukarno's tricks," he told newsmen. But there was another problem to worry about. Back in Malaysia another political storm was blowing with full fury and the reports reaching the Tunku blamed it all on Lee Kuan Yew. According to UMNO stalwarts who had the Tunku's ear, Lee had had the impertinence to challenge one of the most sacred claims of the Malays – that of being *bumiputras*, the indigenous people of Malaya, the sons of the soil. Lee would strenuously deny he had done so. The denials would be ignored.

The Malays were quick to see a sinister motive behind Lee's alleged pronouncements. If the PAP politician started trying to prove they were not the indigenous people of Malaysia, he would soon thereafter be questioning their special economic privileges. Next he would challenge their special political status and its built-in constitutional safeguards. No Malay would tolerate this. Malaysia would then be in very serious trouble.

UMNO leaders decided Lee was clearly courting serious trouble and immediately gave it to him in full measure. Albar roared like an enraged tiger. Syed Nasir, another UMNO strongman, dug up ancient history to prove that the Malays had come to Malaya more than three thousand years earlier. Senu bin Abdul Rahman, Minister of Information and Broadcasting, was furious. He pointed out angrily that nowhere else in the world could migrant races enjoy such prosperity and happiness as in Malaysia. But with men like Lee around, said the minister, it could all go up in flames.

Even Tun Razak, usually cool-headed and soft-spoken, was now steaming with anger. Razak, acting as prime minister in the Tunku's absence, said Lee had created a very serious situation by attacking the Malays.

The Tunku, listening to it all from Japan, found it difficult not to be annoyed with Lee. Why did he have to make such preposterous statements? There had been Malay kingdoms since the earliest recorded history. When the British first arrived in Malaya, they found Malay settlements, with their own hereditary rulers, laws and administration. The treaties with the British had been made by sultans. There were no Lee Kuan Yews around in those days.

This was how the Tunku reasoned: The British had found the old Malaya rich in natural resources and decided to 'protect' it in order to keep its riches to themselves. For all practical purposes Malaya became a British colony. The British had also found that most Malays preferred to work for themselves as farmers and fishermen. Nature was kind to them and gave them a living for little work. It gave them plenty of time for leisure, time to sit back and ponder the meaning of life, and enjoy it with music and dancing and laughter and love.

Many would say that the Malays were lazy, but this wasn't true. They had different values, that was all, simple values designed for an uncomplicated and happy existence. They had no time for the kind of ambition that closed a man's mind to life's pleasures and drove him on in a grim, relentless pursuit of power and wealth.

Life without happiness was meaningless, and happiness could be found watching the sunrise, or the rice fields ripen, in the relaxed company of village friends, with music in the moonlight, or in a woman's bed. All this could be had, the Tunku would assert, without power and wealth.

Magellan's brother-in-law, Duarte Barosa, had visited this area around the 1500s and had said of the Malays: "They are polished and well-bred, fond of music and given to love."

Much later, a British scholar, Sir Richard Winstedt, wrote that the Malays had "a better sense of the values of what life offers than is generally gained from book philosophies". The Malay was usually a man of gentle and courteous ways, but he could also be treacherous if his feelings were hurt or his interests threatened.

The British left the Malays in their rural contentment and allowed migration into the country. Hundreds of thousands of Chinese and Indians soon came to work the rubber estates and tin mines and lay down roads and railways.

The time came when the Malays realised the newcomers had gone ahead of them. Working in the new and expanding industries, the Chinese and the Indians had learned modern techniques and the value of education. For the Malays, time had stood still and they had been left behind in their backwardness. They needed help and protection.

The British again had seen to that. The constitution of 1948 had specified this. This was their land and the Malays were entitled to the rewards of ownership. That was how it stood, whatever Lee Kuan Yew might say.

The Tunku returned from Tokyo on May 11 and found his party much angrier than he had expected. On May 14, at the UMNO annual conference, the delegates were burning with rage. They demanded the immediate arrest of Lee and the banning of the

PAP. They asked that action be taken at once by Dr Ismail, the Minister in charge of internal security. Otherwise there would be bloodshed.

Ismail, dour but stubbornly democratic, refused to give in. He told the delegates that as long as Lee did not step outside the law, it would be wrong to lock him up. As Lee was relying on democratic weapons, UMNO would fight him democratically. And win. Lee might be clever, Ismail told his colleagues, but in every clever person there lay a bit of foolishness. Lee's foolishness was that he had failed to see no one could rule Malaysia without the support of the Malays.

The Tunku reminded the delegates of the fall of former UMNO president, Dato Onn bin Jaafar. Dato Onn had been a much bigger man than Lee, a truly national figure who was widely respected, and, more importantly, a fellow Malay. He had been such a giant of a politician that people had laughed at the Tunku for having agreed to stand against him. But Dato Onn had destroyed himself. After breaking away from UMNO, he began using racial tactics to win support, pretending to be non-racial. That was the end of him.

The Tunku was convinced the Chinese on the peninsula would never support Lee against UMNO. They were a very practical people. They had only to look around and they would see the immense wealth Malaysia had given them. They owned three-quarters of the Malaysian economy. Nearly 70 per cent of all the students in universities at home and abroad were Chinese. Lee would never be able to make the Chinese believe they were not getting a fair deal. On the contrary, his brand of politics would frighten them for it could destroy everything they had achieved.

With great reluctance, UMNO delegates decided to accept the advice of the Tunku and Dr Ismail. But only for the time being! They would wait for another opportunity to settle accounts with Lee. They tracked his every move as he went about setting up a united front to widen his attack.

Lee called it the Malaysian Solidarity Convention and said it would fight for a 'Malaysian Malaysia'. It seemed an innocent enough slogan. But to most Malays it suggested the concealment of something threatening. According to Lee, it simply meant a Malaysia in which all Malaysians – Malays, Chinese, Indians and others – would be equal. But what did that mean? The angry men in UMNO insisted it meant only one thing. Lee wanted to take away the special privileges and the special safeguards of the Malays. And that was not fair! In spite of these privileges and safeguards the Malays were much poorer than the other races. Less than one per cent of them were in business. Less than 15 per cent of all Malaysian students in universities were Malays. If the little that the Malays had was to be taken away from them, what would their future be? In sheer desperation they would turn to the Indonesians for help against Chinese economic oppression and Malaysia would become a tinder box.

The Tunku's men found their opportunity to attack Lee again a few weeks later at the new session of parliament. The King himself opened the session on May 25 with a speech from the throne. It was a harmless speech in which he appealed for national unity to meet the aggression from Indonesia.

For his part, Lee registered his disappointment the King had not assured the nation that steps would be taken to create a Malaysian Malaysia. He also took offence at a statement in the Royal Address that there were enemies within the country. Lee immediately assumed that the King had been referring to the PAP. When a government back-bencher moved a motion of thanks to the King, Lee tried to amend it to express his regret.

His UMNO enemies were delighted. To them, the brilliant Mr Lee had set a trap and walked right into it himself. Country-wide the Malays would strongly resent Lee's attack on the Royal speech. They would be asking: "How dare this Chinese upstart insult our King?" Lee's hopes of winning Malay support were now totally doomed.

They were right in the thick of this battle when Lee made another move that seemed like a huge blunder to his UMNO opponents. One weekend, while Parliament was still in session, he flew back to Singapore to make a speech. He spoke about a Malaysian Malaysia, and added: "The agreement in the constitution must lead to a Malaysian Malaysia, and if they want to stop it they must use unconstitutional methods to stop it. So, I say, if they want to do that – do it now! It will be easier for us to make other arrangements. If that is what they want, we have got other ideas of looking after ourselves. Those states which want a Malaysian Malaysia can get together."

Earlier, while speaking on the same subject Lee was recorded to have said: "If we must have trouble, let us have it now instead of waiting for another five or ten years."

To the angry men in UMNO these statements taken together could mean only one thing. Lee was planning to partition Malaysia! Some of the fiercest battles ever seen in the Malaysian Parliament were fought in the next few days. Lee used all his debating skills to deny the accusations against him, but, to the emotionally charged UMNO men, he seemed to be trapped in a corner of his own making. They spoke of him as having completely exposed his ambitions; a politician who, wanting to carve his place in history, would even wreck Malaysia. What enormous vanity, they pronounced.

Dr Ismail accused Lee of spreading wicked fairy tales about Malaysia. In these tales the backward people of Malaysia, the Malays, were planning to dominate the robust and economically powerful Chinese. Unfortunately, said the Malaysian minister, many foreign correspondents had believed these stories and sent them around the world. During a fiery exchange, Dr Ismail insisted the PAP had two images like the two faces – Dr Jekyll and Mr Hyde. He continued: "These two images cannot remain separate for long. The two must come together. The time for merging must come." As if this was not enough, the internal security chief added: "The PAP is a party that shouts 'fire, fire, fire' but commits arson."

A much sterner warning came from the deputy prime minister. Tun Razak said it was clear Lee was trying to become the champion of the Chinese against the Malays. Since he couldn't have everything his own way, he was determined to break Malaysia in two – into a Malay Malaysia and a Lee Kuan Yew Malaysia. To achieve this he had gathered around him the other opposition parties for whom, in fact, he had the utmost contempt. He had even gone round the world complaining about Malaysia's domestic affairs to the leaders of other countries. Lee had better watch out! The Malays had already been pushed too far. If he kept up this dangerous game, they would react much as they deplored racial violence. The situation could easily get out of hand completely and Lee would be held fully responsible.

The Tunku listened to it all in silence. He was deeply unhappy. He had always dreamed of a 'Happy Malaysia' but the dream was turning into a nightmare. What was happening to his

Dato Dr Ismail bin Dato Abdul Rahman, Malaysia's powerful Minister of Internal Security who angered UMNO extremists when he flatly rejected their demand for the arrest of Lee Kuan Yew.

old friend Harry Lee? The man was now so full of venom that his every word was like a poison dart. The Tunku decided he must not speak in the debate for if he did he would have to attack Lee. With the situation so serious, he must hold himself aloof and above the fray. He must play the role of the Old Man, the Father of Malaysia, to whom all, including Lee, could go with their troubles. He must abandon the usual role he had enjoyed so much as the aggressive leader of his party. He must play the peace-maker.

SECTION 2

Lee Kuan Yew, proud of his humble background and at the same time academically brilliant, was convinced he had all the attributes to be the leader of Singapore. From this position he was determined to help forge a permanent national entity of his island state and the neighbouring Malayan peninsula. This section depicts the separation story from the Singapore viewpoint.

The Trapped Lion

The PAP Trounced

Blood Must Flow

The Unspoken Word

The 'Ultras'

The Unbending Backbone

Nobody in the region could rouse a crowd to a political concept better than Singapore's Lee Kuan Yew seen here in September, 1963, addressing a state election campaign rally at the island's Fullerton Square.

THE TRAPPED LION

As the Tunku lay in the London Clinic battling shingles, Lee Kuan Yew was in Singapore, reflecting on the future of Malaysia. He was an angry and frustrated lion. He was a man of exceptional intellectual power and newspapers in Britain, Australia and even in North America, Europe and the other Asian countries were confirming it for him. He was a dynamic and incorruptible leader. Foreign correspondents in Singapore were telling their readers back home that Lee had gone to Cambridge to study law and achieved the rare distinction of winning a double first. It was also in Britain, they reported, that Harry Lee Kuan Yew became a confirmed socialist.

Lee's oratory was matchless. He never delivered a speech in the conventional way. He always performed it, with skilful use of words and a superb sense of timing. He could annihilate an opponent with his talent for mockery, ridicule and contempt. With a careful selection of facts, he could lay an ambush swiftly and cunningly. Crouching for the final attack, his speech would drop to a near-whisper. Every ear in whatever room or hall it was would be straining for the climax. Then the voice would suddenly expand to a harsh roar, startling everyone.

The Singapore leader could use words gently, soothingly, to sell a difficult point. He could preach a sermon in solemn, ringing tones, or deliver a rebuke like a schoolmaster in language that conveyed hurt and disappointment. He could use phrases to challenge and inspire, or employ them like a surgeon's knife to dissect and analyze the most complex problem. He could speak like a statesman in dignified, arresting language that compelled men to think about the larger issues and look to the future. Or deliver a warning like a thug.

Tunku Abdul Rahman had once said the PAP secretary general could talk the hind legs off a donkey. A London daily had named the Singaporean politician the most entertaining speaker around. If Lee ever lost his job as a politician, it was widely conceded, he would always be able to make a living giving lectures.

Lee Kuan Yew had learned to profit from the presence of foreign correspondents in Singapore. Invariably they preferred to set up offices on the island rather than in Kuala Lumpur. All the important air routes in the region converged on Singapore and this was vital to men who had to be in Hong Kong, Saigon or Jakarta at a moment's notice. Singapore also had better cable facilities. But, most importantly, it had a prime minister who never failed to provide first-rate copy.

Foreign correspondents were simply unable to establish easy working relationships with government leaders in Kuala Lumpur. Journalists sensed a tendency among politicians there to be rigidly dogmatic about things. Probing questions were often resented and ignored. Correspondents who asked them were sometimes suspected of having been set up by Lee to adopt unfriendly attitudes to the Malays in the Federal capital.

On the other hand, Lee seemed to have welcomed such questions. He could often turn them to his advantage with replies that made not only good sense but good newspaper copy. He could always be counted on to produce a pungent phrase that summed up the gist of the most complicated issue – the very nub of headlines. Lee worked at being the master of his subject, accurate to the last detail – which was definitely not the case with the Tunku who could tell a major press conference, without a flicker, that the border with Indonesia was 1, 800 miles long, when in reality it was only 800 miles.

All Lee's accomplishments, however, seemed totally irrelevant to the PAP leader in the face of the problems confronting him in 1965. Malaysia was in trouble, serious trouble, and he felt powerless to prevent the impending disaster. He had always believed Malaya and Singapore should be one. The separation imposed on them by British colonialism was a cruel perversion of history and geography. More than that, it had cut right across family links. There were fathers and mothers and sisters and brothers and cousins on either side of the Causeway, and to those concerned the political separation of Malaya and Singapore made no sense at all.

In September, 1961, in a radio broadcast, Lee told these people: "Merger is going to take place not just because it is the desire of the People's Action Party, or merely because it is the wish of the Alliance Government in Malaya. It is as inevitable as the rising and setting of the sun. The two territories are so inter-twined and interwoven in their economic, political and military complex that no man can keep up the artificial barrier at the Causeway for long. Everyone knows the reasons why Malaya is important to Singapore. It is the hinterland which produces the rubber and tin that keep our shop-window economy going. It is the base that made Singapore the capital city. Without this economic base, Singapore would not survive."

The facts, as Lee saw them, were these.

Merger between Singapore and Malaya would be mutually beneficial. If they remained apart and went their own separate ways, Singapore's economy would begin to decline. Unemployment would increase, giving rise to greater public discontent. The growing unrest would go from bad to worse, playing right into the hands of the communists.

If ever the CPM came to power in Singapore, Malaya would be in grave danger. The Singapore-based communists would set out at once to subvert the Malayan government and the island would become a 'second Cuba'. Despite the official declaration of the end of the Malayan Emergency in 1960, pockets of hard-core communists still existed along the peninsula and the Tunku was determined to contain the damage they could inflict.

The Tunku had already made it clear he would fight back with all the power at his command if Singapore fell to the communists. One could only imagine the measures that would result, the extreme inconveniences and the all round unhappiness of the average citizen living on the island. First, there would be sanctions. Then, perhaps, the water supply from Johore would be cut. It was foolish for anyone to assume the Tunku was too soft to have such moves implemented. So, step-by-step, Malaya and a communist-held Singapore would move towards war, a war that could turn into a racial conflict between Malays and Chinese. The outcome was too terrifying even to contemplate.

Supreme authority in Singapore still lay in the hands of the British. The local political stage of that period was held, as Lee saw it, mostly by 'crooks, clowns and British puppets'. These men functioned in a sterilised chamber, safe from the acute political fever raging in their midst. They played a charmed game for their own profit, and the benefit of the British. They went through forms and motions of democracy, but democracy itself was absent.

Watching all this from below the surface were silent, fierce men who were growing more and more impatient at all the play-acting. They had seen the myth of British superiority blasted by the Japanese and were determined that no one was ever again going to push them around. They could and would govern themselves with self-respect.

The group was made up of liberal-minded politicians, left-wing thinkers and dedicated communists. The three groups were held together by their anti-British sentiments and their mutual objective of pursuing an anti-colonial struggle. The young dynamic Lee Kuan Yew and his colleagues became part of this scene. It seemed to be an expedient, pragmatic move. They knew the day would come when there would be a parting of the ways, that scores would one day be settled, but until that time they would all work together against the British.

On November 21, 1954, Lee and his colleagues set up the PAP and pledged to work for an independent state consisting of Malaya and Singapore. Among those present at its inaugural meeting was Tunku Abdul Rahman, president of Malaya's UMNO. The Tunku wished the new party success and said if there were more men like the PAP leaders, Singapore and Malaya would be united as one country sooner than most people expected.

From its inception, the PAP began to feel the influence and workings of communists who had joined the party. Indeed, in 1957, they nearly wrested contol of the party by packing its annual delegates' conference with their supporters who were not even PAP members. But the communists and their sympathizers had overplayed their hand. The British stepped in and arrested many of their leading members.

The PAP's 1959 election victory, which made Lee Kuan Yew prime minister of Singapore, would prove an extremely valuable preparatory exercise for the party's ultimate showdown with the communists in 1961. By this time, the CPM and its sympathizers were fighting desperately to prevent a merger between Singapore and Malaya. They were well aware their activities had alarmed the Tunku across the Causeway and that the Malayan leader would insist on having control of Singapore's internal security when the island merged with Malaya. They also knew that the Tunku, after his experience with communist insurgents in Malaya, would not hesitate to use harsh measures against their remaining force in Singapore.

When the left-wing realised they could not persuade the PAP to abandon the proposed merger, they broke away to form a new opposition group called the *Barisan Socialis*. The battle for merger intensified sharply. The *Barisan Socialis* and the underground communist movement launched a vicious campaign against the terms for Singapore's union with Malaya. They branded the whole plan a British neo-colonialist plot.

Although weakened by the split, the PAP fought back vigorously and skilfully. It manoeuvred its other anti-communist opponents into a position where they were left with no choice. If they refused to support the PAP, they would be helping the *Barisan Socialis* and the communists.

Lee's view was that Singapore on its own would be doomed. In a referendum called on September 1, 1962, the people gave the merger a convincing nod. There were bitter complaints from the losers that unfair tactics had been employed but, whatever the merits of their charge, there was no doubt Singapore had voted for merger.

The positive result of the referendum was the end of a long and exhausting ordeal for Lee and his colleagues. They felt like men who had run a difficult and exhausting marathon. But the reward was also worth the effort. With luck they could now relax and wait for the day when Singapore would move smoothly and gracefully into its place in the new nation – Malaysia.

Lee fully supported the British proposition to bring Sabah and Sarawak as well into Malaysia, though some of the Tunku's reasons for agreeing to it amused him. The Tunku apparently believed that the people of those states would help in the numbers game. The Malayan prime minister thought the inhabitants in those territories, while neither Malay nor Chinese, would off-set the numbers of the Chinese in Singapore. Lee had a different reading of the situation but decided it was not Singapore's problem, at least, not yet.

Rest and relaxation following the September referendum did not last long. Lee soon had to face a new challenge from the Malayan Finance Minister Tan Siew Sin. As President of the MCA, Tan was excited at the prospects in Singapore. The island's large Chinese community was a vast new field which could be tapped by his party. Tan knew it would not be easy, for the PAP was a formidable opponent and had been there years ahead of him. But he believed he had a powerful weapon that could prove critical in this situation.

This was Tan's belief: the Chinese in Singapore were mainly businessmen or people who depended on some trade or other. These people were always very susceptible to pressures that might affect their vested interests. To him, the Chinese in Singapore, like all entrepreneurial Chinese anywhere, were practical and pragmatic. Tan decided he must show them that as minister of finance in the central government, he could control their fortunes. He was convinced if he did this in a dramatic fashion, the Singapore Chinese would see where their best interests lay and would support him personally as well as his MCA. Tan decided he would play this card when the terms of Singapore's entry into Malaysia came up for further discussion.

In the financial negotiations leading to merger, Lee was shocked at Tan Siew Sin's attitude. First, he wanted 55 per cent of what was regarded as Federal revenue collected in Singapore. To the Singapore prime minister, this was ridiculous – exorbitant beyond belief! This was reduced to 40 per cent, a figure arrived at after much acrimony and churlishness.

Then Lee faced another totally unexpected demand. Discovering that Singapore had over $400 million in reserves, Tan wanted $50 million as a grant to help the economic development in Sabah and Sarawak. It was reported that Lee told the people of Singapore: "Tan opened up our cupboards and found we had money, so he wants $50 million. But this is hard-earned cash, not money from heaven. We are too poor to play Santa Claus. Tan Siew Sin wants the money given to him so that *he* can give it out. He doesn't want it given direct to Sabah and Sarawak because that might make them independent. He wants to line up all the states. He'll drop something in the hats of those he likes. Those he doesn't like, he will tell them to buzz off."

Tan persisted in his demand all the way to London to finalise the Malaysia Agreement. There were many 'ultimatums' and 'final offers' to try to frighten Lee into submission. But Lee had gone to London also determined to fight it out. He reminded Tan that Malaysia without Singapore would be deprived of the sinews to defend herself. If Singapore were kept out of Malaysia, the British bases on the island, so essential to Malaysia's defence, would rapidly disappear.

Finally, for the sake of Malaysia, Lee offered an interest-free loan of $150 million in place of the grant. Tan repaid this gesture by saying, on his return to Malaysia, that Lee had tried to be too clever in London and had made a fool of himself to the tune of $5 million. Instead of agreeing to the grant of $50 million, Lee had given away much more in interest on his loan. "Utter rot," retorted Lee and instructed his government to prove by means of a complicated formula that Tan had got his figures all wrong.

Another tart and peevish incident concerning money cropped up during the London discussions. The British armed forces in Singapore were occupying over four thousand acres of state land without proper titles and Lee decided that something should be done about them. During the London talks, the British Government agreed to return over one thousand acres and pay a cash compensation for the rest. It offered $10 million but Lee wanted $15 million.

Duncan Sandys, now the Commonwealth Relations Secretary leading the British side, was tough. Lee decided he would be twice as exacting. He had been trained in a hard school in Singapore, dealing with communists. They had taught him the value of 'utter and absolute stamina and perseverance'. The negotiations dragged on and on. There were long hours of belligerent debate.

Tunku Abdul Rahman, waiting in London to sign the final agreement, grew impatient. He stepped in and persuaded Lee to accept the British offer. At a press conference that followed his

Singapore celebrates the birth of Malaysia on September 16, 1963, with a gala parade that has its highpoint with a march past a festooned City Hall. There, politicians, dignitaries and guests watch the festivities from a special viewing dais.

assent, Lee explained why he had relented. "If it had not been for the Tunku, we would have had Duncan Sandys on his bended knees, and I want you to quote me on that," he said. "Mind you, we would have preferred to slug it out to the end, but what is $5 million in the history of Malaysia? That was the question the Tunku posed to me. A descendant of a poor peasant allowed himself to be persuaded by a prince of the Royal House of Kedah to give up $5 million on the assurance that all would be well."

Singapore welcomed the birth of Malaysia on September 16, 1963 with an explosion of merry-making that went on for a week. Large crowds were entertained at variety shows and dazzling fireworks lit the night sky. Sixty-seven illuminated floats dressed up to depict various aspects of a vigorous, multi-racial society formed a colourful parade. There was a procession with 100 flag and 500 sparkler-bearers who were followed by children in all the costumes of Malaysia. A float came at the end of it all. It was in the shape of a giant water-lily whose petals burst open in front of the City Hall to reveal five dancing girls. A 500-foot dragon swam along the waterfront, with lights that made it look like an awe-inspiring monster dominating the night scene.

Business turned buoyant. Land prices soared spectacularly and the shares of development companies shot up on the stock exchange. Above the sounds of gaiety and success was the triumphant voice of Lee Kuan Yew fighting an election campaign. Lee had called a general election three days after declaring the independence of Singapore on August 31, 1963.

On September 21, the British Army handed over Fort Canning, its headquarters in Singapore for over a hundred years. On the same day, the people of Singapore went to the polls to elect a new government. They had three choices.

One was the communist-penetrated *Barisan Socialis* which was utterly opposed to Malaysia. It held the promise of a hectic period of extreme political agitation, strikes, riots and economic disruption that was bound to be followed by strong repressive action from the central government.

Another was the Singapore Alliance, a sickly limb of the main Alliance Party. This grouping had hoped Malaysia would give it a transfusion of new, healthy blood. It told voters that the Tunku would be indulgent with Singapore if they respected his wishes and chose an Alliance government. But this resulted in the fear that, in return, Singapore would have to submerge its unique identity and submit to a Malay-dominated central government which tended to treat the Chinese as second-class citizens.

The third choice was Lee's PAP which insisted Singapore must never trust in the charity of anyone. It must never accept the role of a stepchild going to Kuala Lumpur on bended knees for little favours. Singapore had won its proud place as a great international port, as the budding 'New York of Malaysia', not by accident but through the superior skills of its people. Their diligence and endurance, their astuteness in business and a clean, honest and highly efficient government had made Singapore a dynamic place. It deserved a government which had the will and the capacity to stand up and fight, if necessary.

The people of Singapore chose Lee Kuan Yew and gave the PAP its dominant 13-seat parliamentary majority.

THE PAP TROUNCED

Six months after its triumph in the 1963 Singapore elections, the PAP made a momentous decision. The party would enter the broader Malaysian political arena.

As it happened, there were two compelling reasons for Singapore staying out of the 1964 general elections in Malaya. Firstly, while the PAP was superbly organised on the island, it was little more than a name in Malaya. This was a serious handicap. Previous elections had proved that, to ensure victory, a party needed an efficient election machine built on a sound political structure. It needed a network of branches backed up by women and youth movements, and a fleet of hundreds of cars to supplement the limited public transport in most areas.

The second hurdle was the possibility of a hostile reaction from the Malay voters. Most of them had been led to believe the PAP was a Chinese party. They might regard its entry into the election as a new challenge to their special position. This, in turn, could lead to a ganging up of the Malays against the Chinese within the UMNO leadership, with the moderate side losing to dangerous fanatics. Futhermore, because of the electoral strength of the rural Malay vote, the Malays held a commanding position in at least 66 of the 104 constituencies. Most of the seats would go to a party like the Tunku's UMNO. It was an accepted fact that no other party could hope to have a hand in the running of Malaysia unless it worked with the Tunku.

These were the main reasons *against* contesting but there were also reasons *for* competing. If Malaysia was to grow into a strong and healthy nation, it must break out of its prison of racial politics and create a new environment in which men could seek their fulfillment free of narrow prejudices and fears. The Alliance, with its emphasis on separate parties for the Malays, Chinese and Indians was strengthening the walls between them. It was constantly reminding the various racial groups of their separateness. As the main messenger of non-racial politics, the PAP must penetrate those walls and help the willing to knock them down. It could not afford to confine itself to its achievements within the limits of a tiny island.

The PAP had been noting an encouraging trend on the mainland. In one major town after another where the voters were mainly non-Malays, the Alliance had been losing ground to parties like the Socialist Front and the People's Progressive Party, both of which claimed to be non-racial. This could mean the urban areas of Peninsular Malaysia, like Singapore, were now ready for the PAP brand of politics. It could also mean that an Alliance partner, Tan Siew Sin's MCA, was losing its grip on these areas.

To Lee this was not surprising. As far as he was concerned, the MCA had become a disgrace and was widely held in contempt. Far from representing the political aspirations of the Chinese, it had become a haven for influence peddlers and men who used the Alliance to promote their own business interests.

Around this time, the 'Ali-Baba' arrangement thrived. Ali, the influential Malay politician with no money, would use his special privileges to get a licence, or a government contract, or land concessions or some other form of favoured treatment. He would get together with Baba, the Chinese businessman with money to spare, and together they would set up a new company in Ali's name. Baba would finance the whole undertaking in which Ali would be given a directorship, free of charge. With Ali's political pull and Baba's business connections they would make a fortune very rapidly. In this process, some curious men from the MCA had risen to high political positions and had become a bane on Malaya's political life.

UMNO had pledged to use the special privileges of the Malays to help improve the economic position of large depressed sections within the Malay community. The Ali-Baba syndrome, however, had done no more than create a small class of Malay elite. Most of them were prominent politicians who had become directors of several firms and were quite rich. But, in the rural areas, life for the average Malay peasant or fisherman was not much better than it had been for his father and his grandfather. Despite this, his loyalty to UMNO had remained intact. For this was the party that had won *Merdeka*, had made Malay the National Language and Islam, the official religion. One day, perhaps, the rural Malay would become impatient for the better life and begin to realise the remedy lay in an economic rather than a racial approach to the problem. That day seemed still a long way off.

To the astute observer, the urban areas presented a different picture. There were obvious signs of more prosperity and a building boom, but discontent was rising among the non-Malays. The Constitution guaranteed them equality but they could see discrimination all around them. A brilliant Chinese schoolboy at the top of his class could lose the government scholarship to a mediocre Malay classmate. A non-Malay candidate applying for a government position could be by-passed in favour of a Malay with lower qualifications, or find himself barred altogether by a quota system favouring Malays.

On this uneven playing field, the MCA did no more than appeal to the non-Malays for tolerance and a spirit of compromise. It held the condescending view that the Malays were playing with power like children with a new toy and would soon grow tired of it. Better to put up with a little discrimination than to resist and risk a violent upheaval. The price the MCA had to pay for this stand was a steady loss of urban votes to parties like the Socialist Front. They were strengthening the left-wing hand!

Lee Kuan Yew had an additional reason for anxiety. Since 1955, the predominantly-Malay government of Malaya had been faced with the problem of communist subversion in schools, trade unions and political parties. The communists were nearly all Chinese. The police, the armed forces and the civil service, manned mainly by Malays, were accustomed to using harsh measures in dealing with Chinese offenders, but they were not always able to tell the difference between communist subversion and genuine Chinese grievances. As a result, the battle for the hearts and minds of the Chinese was being lost, and the situation was getting steadily worse.

The new cadres being recruited by the communists were tough, well-educated, highly-motivated young men, far superior to their predecessors who had been semi-literate peasants and workers. Using the big stick against these men would be playing right into their hands. They must be fought with tactics as subtle and intelligent as their own, like those the PAP had used so successfully in Singapore.

Lee's PAP decided it had more than a reason, *it had a duty* to contest the 1964 election. The Socialist Front was Sukarno's advance guard in Malaysia and must be deprived of any protest votes against the MCA and the Alliance. The PAP – offering leadership with a strong backbone, an effective response to the communist challenge, and 'Democratic Socialism' – would have a good chance of succeeding as it had done in Singapore. But it must be careful. It must not give extremist Malay elements any excuse to tell the rural Malays that the Chinese in the towns were making a bid for power. This could well open the door for pro-Indonesian leaders to take over UMNO and cooperate with Jakarta to 'fix' the Chinese.

To prevent any misunderstanding, the PAP opted only for a token entry into the Malayan election. The party took great care to make its position absolutely clear, explaining that it had no intention of challenging UMNO to form the central government. It would stand only in those areas where there was a danger of the Socialist Front gathering protest votes against the MCA. To prove its sincerity, the PAP withdrew two of its eleven candidates on Nomination Day when it discovered they were opposed by UMNO men.

Lee also made it plain he intended to put across the 'democratic socialism' of the PAP, with its non-racial approach to the problems of economic development and a fair distribution of wealth. He was sure that if his limited effort in the Malayan election was successful, 'winds of change' would begin to sweep throughout Malaysia and the Alliance would feel obliged to adopt some of the policies of the PAP. Eventually he hoped to win enough support among the urban voters to force UMNO to reconsider its position and accept a new and more enlightened partnership with the PAP. At best the prospect was still some years away, but Lee was willing to wait.

The Singapore leader was stunned by the Tunku's sharp rejection of any cooperation with the PAP. Instead the Malaysian prime minister made his famous pledge that the Alliance partners would all swim or sink together. Equally shocking was the Tunku's accusation that Lee had said, in an election speech delivered in Chinese, that the Tunku did not have the calibre to lead the nation. The obvious insinuation was that Lee was attacking UMNO in Chinese (a language UMNO couldn't understand) while praising it in English (a language it could).

The allegation, based on information from the MCA, was completely untrue. Lee had never made any such statement about the Tunku. But the charge was to haunt him right through the election campaign, repeated by one Alliance leader after another to incite the Malays against him. This went on despite his denials and despite his challenge that they should check the police recording of his speech.

Lee told an election rally that he was deeply saddened by the Tunku's remarks. He added: "My colleague, the Minister for Culture (Othman Wok) was present when the Tunku read from a written script at the rally. He told me over the phone that it was a pity the Tunku should have been dragged into the thing. They should never have brought him down to this level, putting such stuff in his speech. One of the most endearing features of the Tunku is his staunch personal loyalty to his old friends."

Half the problems that Malaysia faced had been created by the Tunku's old friends who skilfully and cynically exploited his personal loyalties.

Lee tried hard to repair the damage. He assured the Malays that as far as he was concerned, all Malaysians were in the same boat and there were no better hands to guide the helm than those of the Tunku and his deputy. The PAP only wanted to help in the navigation by pointing out the rocks and perils ahead.

His efforts failed.

As the election campaign wore on, the MCA began to hit back viciously at the PAP through UMNO. Senior UMNO leaders were instigated to direct some of their fire constantly at Lee, accusing him of trying to drive a racial wedge between the urban and the rural people. Malay extremists seized the opportunity to strangle the infant hopes just growing among the non-Malays for more equality. Jaafar Albar warned Lee and his supporters: "Don't push the Malays too far."

In the meantime, the Alliance deftly rode the enormous anti-Sukarno wave which Lee himself had helped to unleash. It painted a terrifying picture of Indonesian aggression and fully exploited the fear that this caused. At the same time it offered hopes of an early peace: "Confrontation will automatically disappear if the Alliance wins a big victory, for then Sukarno will realise that the people are fully behind the Tunku."

Lee tried to caution voters against false hopes, for he was convinced that confrontation would go on whatever the results of the election; but it was too late. The tidal wave he had helped to start was now bearing down on him and would soon overwhelm the PAP. He tried desperately to make the people see the need for new men with new policies that would strengthen Malaysia against Sukarno and the communists.

Lee did not begrudge the Tunku credit for the Alliance's great victory in 1964. He was a logical, far-sighted politican. He accepted the win could not have been better for Malaysia as far as international opinion was concerned. Now, no one could doubt the will of the people of Malaysia.

There was, of course, the downside. While in the process of generating a wave of patriotism that helped the Alliance win, the PAP itself was swamped. The party won only one seat, the constituency of Bungsar where a former Singapore political detainee, Devan Nair, won by a narrow margin of 808 votes.

BLOOD MUST FLOW

More than a hundred years ago, a noted Malay writer, Munshi Abdullah, found himself amazed at the energy of the Chinese in Singapore. He wrote: "They build houses as if they were at war."

Abdullah would have been as impressed with Lee Kuan Yew's Singapore in the 1960s. Under the PAP government, huge rectangular blocks of flats were springing up everywhere. It was said Singapore was building flats at the rate of one every 45 minutes! That amounted to ten thousand flats a year. They were building them fast and building them cheaply. It was a dizzying reality. Visitors from Kuala Lumpur saw rows upon rows of large pastel-coloured boxes whiz past their train or bus windows. Inevitably, during their visit, they would be informed by their hosts that most of the people living in these new units had once inhabited slums.

In 1964, the Crawford area in Singapore was 90 acres of filth and squalor crying out for improvement. The overcrowded flimsy houses were more than a hundred years old and needed attention. The place was a ghastly sore on Singapore's face. The population numbered about 2,000 Chinese families and some 200 Malay families.

The PAP government were not neglecting the Crawford area. In fact, plans were afoot to 'rejuvenate' it. The old houses were to be demolished to make way for new dwellings. The homeowners were being offered compensation and given three months to move to places allocated to them elsewhere. As soon as they left, bulldozers were scheduled to move in and then the builders would

In 1964 the Crawford area of Singapore was 90 acres of squalor. Today Crawford Bridge remains as does bustling Crawford Street running across it. But the overall ambience of the district is vastly different.

do their job. Soon Crawford would be a much improved settlement of brick and concrete giants containing many hundreds of new flats. The old residents would be allowed to return, if they wished.

As these plans were being finalised, the PAP government began to sense an ominous mood of unrest among the Malays of Crawford. An unsettling current of rumours of Malays losing out to the Chinese was snaking its way through the normally placid waters of their existence. Lee Kuan Yew watched the rising emotional tension with growing anxiety. He had reason to worry. The disturbing development was affecting Malays in other parts of the island as well.

The rumours had to be stopped but he must first discover their source. It was clear to Lee that groups of Malay extremists were hard at work spreading the poison. Behind them were other men, and discreet enquiries confirmed the suspicion that some of them were leading figures in the Singapore branch of UMNO. These men were reacting to the bitterness of their failure in the 1963 election. They were driven by a blinding hate.

These extremists preferred to stick to their version of history which was a book of painful memories. They remembered Singapore as having once been a Malay state, ruled by a sultan. They carried remembrances of his tomb, a patch of sacred ground on Forbidden Hill, with its prayer house and a caretaker. They claimed the spirit of the sultan was still a strong presence among them. They liked recalling how the British had come to Singapore only much, much later. And then the Chinese in their hundreds of thousands were encouraged to come, workers and traders who eventually took over the island.

When the merger happened on September 16, 1963, the concept had held out a promise to the extremists. They thought Malay dominance in Kuala Lumpur could be extended to Singapore! But it was not working that way. The island still had a Chinese prime minister and his party had even stolen Malay votes from UMNO. Pointedly, in the 1963 election, five days after Malaysia came into being, Lee's party had defeated UMNO candidates even in Malay areas.

The extremists were now saying the spirit of the old sultan was crying out for vengeance. The Malays of Singapore must be shaken out of their slumber. If they could be roused to action, real flaming action, the central government in Kuala Lumpur would be forced to intervene. It would take over Singapore and Malay rule would be restored! To achieve this, the Malays must be made to see that Lee Kuan Yew was against their race. They must be shown that he was now starting to move against them. Look at Crawford! He was driving them from their homes, driving them into the sea. Then he would make the Chinese move in and take over whatever little land was left to them in Singapore. The Malays must stand up and fight or their race would perish from the island.

These were the rumours that were agitating the Malays of Singapore. But there was another dangerous factor.

Across the sea, in Jakarta, Sukarno was screaming out his threat to 'Ganyang Malaysia – Crush Malaysia! He boasted Malaysia would be destroyed by the following New Year's Day. His saboteurs were sneaking into Singapore from islands only an hour or two away by small boat, carrying with them deadly explosives. Their murderous gadgets, exploding in public places, were maiming and killing innocent people.

Even more alarming than these bombs was the vicious propaganda being churned out by Radio Indonesia. It was being broadcast daily from Jakarta and half a dozen other stations.

Sukarno had first addressed himself to the Chinese in Singapore. He warned Malaysia was a plot to bring them under Malay control and oppression. He claimed the Tunku had once whispered to him that the only reason for dragging Sabah and Sarawak into Malaysia was to 'over-vote' the Chinese in Singapore. Indeed, Sukarno never grew tired of telling this story.

But the Chinese in Singapore were not fooled by Sukarno's professed 'concern' for them. They could never forget he was the same man who had been completely heartless with Chinese in his own country. In 1960, he had signed a decree preventing them from doing business in the rural areas of Indonesia. Overnight, tens of thousands found their businesses liquidated. Deprived of their livelihood and property, they were forced to leave the rural areas. Those reluctant to go faced brutality. Countless fearful stories were told and re-told.

Sukarno's pretence was too transparent to have any effect on the Chinese in Singapore. He soon abandoned the attempt.

He turned to the Malays. His propaganda now became an hysterical anti-Chinese tirade. He began to incite the Malays to rise against the Chinese in defense of their race and religion. He exploited the Crawford affair to the hilt.

Indonesian announcers, their voices trembling with passion, were reciting verses from the Holy Koran to justify violence. Grim-voiced commentators were inventing highly provocative incidents. ". . . an old Malay woman, feeble and almost blind, fell of a bus in Orchard Road this afternoon because the Chinese bus driver refused to stop for her. As she lay groaning beside the road, Chinese passers-by laughed and spat at her . . ."

The air was filled with filthy stories, many of them obscene. They could only be fabrications delivered by depraved minds. It was evident what Sukarno was trying to do. If he could start trouble between the Malays and the Chinese in Singapore, it could quickly spread to the mainland, and Malaysia would destroy itself in a civil war.

Lee watched anxiously as temperatures steadily rose. He appealed to the Tunku to defuse the situation by restraining the wild men in Singapore's UMNO. But the tension continued to rise. Finally, Lee himself decided to speak directly to the Malays in Singapore, to reassure them. He invited 114 non-political Malay organisations for a July 19, 1964, meeting.

There is a saying about waving a red flag before a raging bull. This would apply to the reaction of Syed Jaafar Albar. He hated Lee with a burning hate. Albar was proud to be Lee's most deadly enemy. He saw the conflict as a fight to the finish between Malays and Chinese, between UMNO and the PAP. The Chinese leader, ambitious and arrogant, was challenging the power of the Malays. Albar's immediate objective was to smack the PAP leader down hard.

Albar was a superlative speaker in the Malay language. His tongue could be a poison-tipped kris, the weapon of ancient Malay warriors. In the past, the UMNO Secretary General had slain many political foes in verbal battles. He now directly targeted Lee Kuan Yew. For weeks Albar's vitriolic message had been carried into Malay homes by the Malay newspaper *Utusan Melayu* – the Voice of the Malays.

He, too, called a mass meeting in Singapore, inviting 150 Malay organisations to this occasion. He set the date for July 12 – exactly a week before Lee's scheduled gathering. Hundreds packed the small movie theatre and overflowed onto the five-foot-way and the road. Among them were members of the Peninsula Malay Union (PMU). Twelve weeks earlier, the central government in Kuala Lumpur had accused the PMU of recruiting agents for Indonesian terrorism. As the July 12 meeting was about to begin, a mysterious explosion occurred a few miles away – the work, it was speedily decided, of Indonesian saboteurs.

Albar was at his roaring best. He thundered against Lee, hinting that the Singapore politician was conspiring with Mao Tse-Tung against the Malays. Every slashing attack was cheered wildly. The crowd applauded his blunt warning that any Malay who attended the meeting with Lee would be a traitor to his race. "If Lee Kuan Yew wants to make amends, he must consult us as true Malays," Albar declared. At this same meeting, an Action Committee was set up to fight for Malay rights in Singapore. Among its members was a man who had been described by the central government as a 'close Indonesian agent'.

Lee's meeting on July 19 was attended by over a thousand people from 101 Malay organisations. Many carried placards saying: "We want Lee Kuan Yew, not Albar." For five hours, Lee answered questions, gave assurances and explained his government's policies. His ministers and government experts were at hand to assist him.

The Singapore PM explained that his government was not anti-Malay. As a proof, the predominantly Chinese island of Singapore had willingly adopted Malay as its national language. He told them why he could not agree to special quotas for Malays in jobs, business licences, taxis and so on. Such handouts would never get anybody out of poverty. The root problem was education. Too few Malays went to secondary schools, even fewer to universities. Most seemed content with a primary education, leaving them unqualified for better jobs. This had to be changed if the Malays wished to catch up with the other races.

Lee's belief was in further education for the Malays and training them to compete on equal terms with non-Malays. It was the only decent and honourable solution – the only solution. Lee said his government was ready to give the Malays every possible assistance in education. In fact it had already offered them free education right up to university level.

The discussions at the July 19 gathering were serious, restrained and calm. A village leader later said the meeting was 'a model of democracy in action'. There was every reason to be pleased with the outcome.

But two days later, on July 21, came the horrible eruption. For the first time in its history, Singapore was seeing riots between Malays and Chinese. There had been Chinese riots before, and Malay riots as well, but never a clash like this. Early that afternoon, twenty-five thousand Malays had gathered in the *padang*, to commemorate the birthday of the Prophet Mohamed. There, apart from paying religious homage and reciting prayers, organisers had included in their programme a number of fiery and emotional speeches. By the time their procession started to move, agitation had already been stirred and the moderates in the crowd smelled trouble.

Later, according to Lee Kuan Yew in a radio broadcast, a policeman had asked a few stragglers to rejoin the procession. The law enforcer was attacked by them, triggering a disturbance that spread quickly to other areas. Lee also said: "What or who started this situation is irrelevant at the moment. All the indications show that there has been organisation and planning behind this outbreak to turn it into an ugly communal clash. All that was needed was someone to trigger it off."

Deputy Prime Minister of Malaysia Tun Razak, who was also deputy leader of UMNO, flew to Singapore to help quell the trouble. He later told reporters the riots were initially caused by an unknown mischief-maker who had thrown a bottle at the procession.

The Tunku, at the time, was on his goodwill visit to the United States and had just arrived in Williamsburg, Virginia. He could not believe the news from home. "This is one of the unhappiest moments in my life," he said. In a television interview in Washington, he claimed Indonesia was behind the riots. His instinctive response was to dash back but was prevailed upon by Tun Razak to continue with his journey.

Immediately after the July, 1964, Singapore riots, Malaysia's then Acting Prime Minister Tun Abdul Razak flies in for an on-the-spot inspection of crisis areas. He is shown here at the island's airport with Singapore Prime Minister Lee Kuan Yew and Finance Minister Dr Goh Keng Swee.

For nearly twelve hours ugly scenes were replicated in Singapore. Isolated violence continued for several days. Innocent people going about their business or returning home from work were attacked, hardly knowing why. Shops were destroyed, cars overturned and burned.

The toll: 23 dead; 465 injured.

The Singapore Chinese Chamber of Commerce (SCCC) building in Hill Street.

The ornate entrance to the SCCC premises featuring the stone lions fashioned in China.

THE UNSPOKEN WORD

The riots left Lee Kuan Yew in a sombre but undaunted mood. One thing was undeniable – for the present, the political temperature had to be lowered. Still, Lee was also determined no one should be allowed to forget the lessons of the recent tragedy.

Already, in Kuala Lumpur, there were signs the lessons were being ignored. Leaders in the Federal capital were blaming the riots on gangsters and Indonesian agents, on misunderstandings and emotional grievances. Slowly but surely an accusing finger, still concealed behind a screen of goodwill, was shifting. Its target: the PAP.

The lessons were painfully obvious. Anyone looking for an excuse for the riots could easily find a gangster or an Indonesian agent, or a burning grievance. These, to Lee, were only the sparks that set off the explosion. The explosive fuel had been supplied by other men from Kuala Lumpur – men who used the Malay newspaper *Utusan Melayu* as their main propaganda pipeline. These spoilers had been at their mischief for months and no one in Kuala Lumpur had tried to stop them.

"I saw trouble coming three months ago," remarked Lee before reporters. "Every day an insidious line was fanned. Small flames were sparked off and Bukit Mertajam went up in racial riots. Still they did not stop and I was astounded. Then it happened here in Singapore. Can you imagine what it will be like if it happens simultaneously up and down the country?"

He thought it was best for Malaysia that the troublemaking by these men and the methods they employed be exposed and censured.

Lee, who definitely had Albar in mind, demanded a commission of inquiry to examine not merely the 'sparks' but also the basic causes of the riots and how to prevent them. The Tunku, anxious to protect his fierce lieutenant, advised Lee that it would be dangerous to adopt this approach so soon after all the trouble. An inquiry would have to wait until a safer time.

A commission was appointed weeks later, headed by a judge, to hold a closed inquiry. The decision was reached after a cabinet meeting in Kuala Lumpur. Months after its appointment, Lee was to complain that it had yet to do its job.

Meanwhile, the present situation demanded utmost restraint. Lee became extremely careful with his tongue, and whenever he spoke now his words were carefully chosen and spelled moderation and goodwill. This must have been extremely difficult because he still had the message about mischief-makers and the ultimate interests of Malaysia to put across. Its clarity had to be preserved whatever the choice of words or the changes in style might be.

There were needling little provocations all the time from his opponents who now hid behind the Tunku and sniggered at him. This rankled and for a normally pugnacious politician who did not entertain undeserved barbs lightly, the exercise must have been extraordinarily trying. But to his credit Lee persevered and when the Tunku visited Singapore soon after his return from his overseas tour, Lee even stepped aside for him.

On August 20, 1964, the Malaysian prime minister, accompanied by Lee, toured some of the more 'sensitive' areas that still bore the scars of the July riots. Addressing the people in Geylang Serai after the Tunku's reassuring words, Lee spoke of his faith in the Alliance leader. "If we rely only on constitutional and legal rights and obligations, then I say there is little hope for the success of Malaysia," Lee said. "It has got to rest on more than that – on faith and trust. We have accepted the Tunku not just as leader of the Malays but also as the leader of all the races in Malaysia. Otherwise we would not have embarked on Malaysia."

When the second riots erupted on September 2, Lee was attending the Socialist International centenary celebrations in Brussels. Like the Tunku who was in America during the July riots, he did not rush home. While the Tunku was assured by Tun Abdul Razak by radiophone that everything was under control, Lee, on his own, decided against a frantic return journey home. Who would listen to speeches in Singapore at this time? The chaos had taken its own momentum and would eventually dissipate. A determined police force was needed, not an eloquent politician. It was wiser to go on with his plans. From Belgium he went to England for talks with British politicians, including the head of the Labour opposition party, Harold Wilson. Wilson would soon become prime minister and Lee deftly briefed him and his colleagues on Indonesia's *konfrontasi* and other issues that plagued Malaysia.

It was a fruitful trip that would serve Lee in good stead with the Harold Wilson government but this was all in the near future. The present had other things for him. His homecoming in the second week of September, 1964, soon deflated the positive mood that resulted from his meetings in Brussels and London.

Lee returned to a riot-torn island. Tension was palpable. The presence of riot police and plain-clothes men underlined the signs of nervousness among the people. To make matters worse, his fellow leaders in the PAP appeared just as alarmed. The sudden declaration of a curfew had thrown students and office workers in a panic and the ensuing mad rush only added to the fear that spread quickly and unabated.

The Chinese businessmen were naturally running scared. They felt demoralized, absolutely unsettled. The two recent riots had marred their expectations of a happy gathering on September 20, the day the new premises of the Singapore Chinese Chamber of Commerce (SCCC) in Hill Street were to be inaugurated.

Fifty-eight years earlier – in 1906 – a small group of pioneering traders had got together to form the SCCC. It grew, octopus-like, into an extremely powerful organisation whose tentacles reached out into every business sphere of life on the island and beyond. By 1964, its 3,000 members included men who had started out as small shopkeepers but were now international merchants. A number had branched out to become big industrial magnates with connections around the world. These were men who, in 24 hours, could meet a rice shortage in the Philippines with supplies from Thailand, or buy vast quantities of raw rubber from Indonesia, process it and sell it to Europe. They were shrewd, hard men with guts and ability and no political leader in Singapore could afford to ignore them.

In 1911, the SCCC had bought an ancient building dating back to the 19th century. It had a façade that resembled a Chinese temple. The SCCC functioned from this base for many happy and profitable years but by the 1950s, the limited space and the 'antiquated' structure no longer matched the group's achievements and ongoing aspirations.

As the Fifties drew to a close, the SCCC decided to build itself a new home and its various committees set about doing it in their usual high-powered, efficient way. Two and a half million dollars were raised within four years – a whacking achievement by any standard in those days. The ancient house was pulled down and in its place rose a magnificent ten-storey modern building.

The new SCCC was designed to be a landmark to dominate Hill Street and its surroundings; not merely by its size, but also by its striking architectural features. It had a double-tiered roof built in the style of ancient Chinese palaces. In front of the building stood an exquisite chamber that also had a palace-like roof – only considerably smaller and single-tiered. Large stone lions stood on either side of the entrance; though, in truth, no real lion would have ever recognised them. The two statues, separately configured and each balancing a large stone marble, had been shipped all the way from China. A Chinese would touch the marbles for luck. Ironically, in a rare show of diplomacy, Mohammed Khir Johari, the Malaysian Minister of Agriculture, did just that when he visited the building shortly after its inauguration.

Two low walls on either side of the SCCC gate were decorated with glittering murals, each thirty feet long and five feet high. Made of glazed tiles from China, each mural featured nine colourful dragons. Misty clouds floated above the dragons' heads and their tails were lost in a heaving sea to give them an air of mystery.

The new SCCC edifice became a showcase of Chinese success. Pedestrians stopped to admire it and tourists captured it in countless photographs. Everyone remarked on its uniqueness. It was ancient China blended with the modern West in a creation that had no equal in Southeast Asia. It was a proud monument to Chinese qualities of thrift, hard work and ambition.

Lee Kuan Yew was invited to inaugurate the new SCCC home. He appreciated more than ever the need to boost the morale of the entrepreneurs and businessmen who felt uncertain about their future. As always, Lee's oratorical gift saw him rise to the occasion. The Singapore PM delivered a speech that was brilliant, profound and conciliatory.

However, in another part of Singapore, almost to the hour, other sentiments were being aired.

The Tunku was speaking at a reception hosted by the Singapore Alliance. The Malaysian leader advised his audience to be cautious in their approach to communal differences, to be mild, even-tempered. He spoke about setting up peace committees. He sounded like a kindly father telling his children to behave and help save the sanctity of the home. The Tunku rallied the Singapore Alliance leaders: "Strengthen your organisation because the people of Singapore want you to lead them along the path to unity with the rest of Malaysia. They are fed up with all these giddy and stupid politics which do not take into account the happiness, well-being and harmony of the people."

But. he also mentioned other things. He told the Alliance: "This trouble in Singapore was manufactured by Sukarno and I have proof of it. Unfortunately, some politicians in Singapore have not been free from blame. They have created an atmosphere which could be of help to Sukarno in his plan to wreck our society."

The Tunku added: "It is most unfortunate that some of the leaders of Singapore have been inclined to lay emphasis on the differences of race. There is an undercurrent to contest my leadership of the Malaysian people by trying to make out that I am a leader of the Malays only." The key words were unspoken but his meaning was clear to his listeners. Lee Kuan Yew was now challenging his leadership.

The News from Radio Singapore, borrowing its style from the BBC, presented the two speeches in stark, brutal contrast. The following day, Lee said he was carefully studying the implications of what the Tunku had said.

Nearly a week later, on September 25, the Tunku invited Lee to Kuala Lumpur for a heart-to-heart talk. They met and agreed, together with some of their senior colleagues, on a two-year truce. After lengthy discussions, Lee sent immediate instructions to his lieutenants in Kuala Lumpur to hold their fire. They were not to extend their activities to new areas. For two years the Alliance and the PAP would conserve their strength against Sukarno.

But the anti-Lee, anti-PAP partisans inside UMNO had other plans. Within a month of the truce agreement, Mohammed Khir Johari was in Singapore to open five new UMNO branches. He announced to an enthusiastic gathering that the Singapore Alliance was being reorganised and strengthened to fight the PAP in the next elections. "I am confident that we will win enough votes to form the next government of Singapore," he told his jubilant audience. To newspaper reporters who reminded him of the truce, Khir Johari affected innocence and surprise. What truce?

In Kuala Lumpur, the press tackled the Tunku who laughed: "Ah, but Khir Johari doesn't know about that!" In any case, he virtually justified Johari's move. The Tunku said that as far as he was concerned the truce only covered racial issues, and he could see nothing wrong in carrying out a little 'house cleaning' in the Singapore Alliance.

But Khir Johari had flung down a challenge. He had talked about inter-party rivalry and said he could well understand Lee's concern at the growing strength of the Singapore Alliance. "However, that is an occupational hazard any party must be prepared to accept in a cheerful way," he stated dismissively.

The fighter in Lee accepted the development with sheer delight. He said he really preferred the open contest of ideas. His opportunity came exactly one month later, on November 25, at the Budget Session of Parliament. Malaysia's Minister of Finance Tan Siew Sin had decided to try out some new ideas in taxation and stood exposed as a tempting target.

Budget day was supposed to have been Tan's moment of glory. For weeks prior to his Budget address, he had kept both sides of the Causeway guessing. He enjoyed their mixed curiosity and anxiety. Businessmen, office workers and housewives had examined his every utterance, searching for clues to what he would present in parliament. If Tan Siew Sin smiled, it could start a small wave of optimism and the ripples were felt in the stock exchange. If he scowled the wave reversed.

At half-past-two in the afternoon of November 25, Tan strode into a crowded session of parliament and sensed the sudden surge of excitement. He looked pleased with himself. He had his Treasury officials hanging back in the corridors, armed with the new customs regulations that would come into force immediately he announced them at four o'clock.

The Minister of Finance began slowly and deliberately. He delivered pronouncements on international trade and the economic health of the United States, Britain, Germany, Japan and other trading partners of Malaysia. Then he introduced a contrasting note, a warning to the nation that although Malaysia was doing well, it faced a tough future.

Tan paused for a sip of water and surveyed his audience. By this time, many minds had gone wandering off on dream adventures. His eyes darted to the clock and he saw it was time to unzip his bag of secrets. They came tumbling out – a new turnover tax, a payroll tax, a capital gains tax. The wandering minds were slapped to attention by one shock after another.

Lee and his colleagues listened in silence, obviously amazed at some of the new tax proposals. After the session, they dashed back to Singapore the very same evening and spent the weekend scrutinizing every detail of Tan's budget with their experts. Every fact was weighed, every figure measured, every argument analyzed.

When they returned to Kuala Lumpur, the PAP unleashed an attack such as the Malaysian Parliament had never witnessed before. They questioned every assumption, challenged Tan's figures and scoffed at his theories. They were all firing under expert direction and hitting where it hurt. The old days were gone when Tan could sit back and watch the shells falling short, raising harmless clouds of dust.

There was a time when all Tan had to contend with were simple complaints and proposals, most of them from Alliance back-benchers. Complaints, for example, about a village bridge that was too narrow, so that girls crossing it were forced to brush against boys coming from the other side. Good Muslims were not prepared to put up with this kind of inconvenience! There had been a proposal to import wild animals from Africa and let them loose in the jungles of Malaysia to increase the meat supply in rural areas. There had been endless little complaints about the shortage of schoolteachers and village mosques, about bus services and salary scales for office-boys. Never before had there been anything like the PAP onslaught.

Ipoh lawyer, D. R. Seenivasagam, leader of
the People's Progressive Party (PPP), one
of Malaysia's opposition groupings. His
verbal outbursts during local parliamentary
sessions became legendary.

This was just a sampling of the PAP's battle of ideas. But Lee, directing the attack, began to detect a change of mood on the government benches. At first the UMNO politicians had listened to him in amazement. Never before had they seen such a display of power and skill with words. It was sheer pleasure just to listen to him, and they listened as though hypnotized, in absolute silence.

The attitude changed. Soon the same leaders grew suspicious of a man who could attack one of them with such finesse and incisiveness, and hold them fascinated. A deep hostility began to rise among the UMNO line-up and they met Lee's sharp logic with impatience and anger.

But UMNO acerbity towards the Singapore prime minister was not spewed immediately. His detractors directed their aggression first to other opponents. The honour of being their first victim went to D.R. Seenivasagam of the People's Progressive Party, an opposition lawyer with an acid tongue. When he rose to enquire about the activities of a government minister who had been forced to resign, an Alliance back-bencher, Tahir bin Abdul Majid, intervened.

Tahir: "Sit down."

Seenivasagam: "You sit down."

Tahir: "Shut up."

Seenivasagam: "You shut up."

From the government back-benches came a loud chorus of voices and then a sharp exchange of abuse.

"Stupid ass."

"Bastard."

"Son of a bitch."

"Pariah."

Suddenly a book flew across the chamber in the direction of Seenivasagam. It was a copy of the Standing Orders of Parliament!

The following day, Seenivasagam took the floor again on another subject. He felt the Prime Minister, the Tunku, "should have had more sense" than to appoint as Attorney-General a man whose wife was a government back-bencher.

The Minister of Transport, Sardon bin Haji Jubir – a heavy man with popping eyes and a booming voice – rose to object to what he regarded as an unparliamentary remark about the prime minister.

Seenivasagam: "Clean your ears."

Sardon: "I have cleaned my ears."

Seenivasagam: "Clean them hard then."

There were more shouts of "sit down" and "bastard" from the government back-benches.

Lee, sitting a few feet away from Seenivasagam, found it a highly unedifying spectacle and chided the lawyer. There was no doubt Seenivasagam had been baited and provoked a little too far, but at least he should have watched his language. Lee could not know it then, but he too would face the same treatment before long. In the meantime, his mind was on other thoughts.

Late one night, after many hot words had been exchanged by his fellow parliamentarians, Lee made one of his best speeches in the Malaysian Parliament. He spoke very quietly and very appealingly, with words that were soft and persuasive.

He told members of the House of a trend that was causing him grave anxiety. There seemed to be a growing intolerance, both inside and outside Parliament, of free debate and discussion. Any new idea that did not conform to the established order of things was immediately stifled and buried. Any person who had the courage to challenge the Alliance philosophy and propose new concepts had to face a barrage of 'vilification and vituperation'.

Outside Parliament, he said, the government-controlled radio and television – and particularly the Malay-language newspaper *Utusan Melayu* – were carrying out a campaign of hate, abuse and falsehoods. It was souring the whole nation.

The same techniques were also being used inside Parliament, he pursued, though not by big men like the Tunku. There were gentle, liberal leaders who would not make a move or say a word to spoil their image. But behind them sat hatchet-men, ready to do the dirty work. These were the tough guys who would try to drown every new idea in a sea of hysterical abuse, racial prejudices and hate.

The time had come, said Lee, to ask if Malaysia believed in an open society where men could test their opinions in open encounters, and truth could be refined in the exchange of different views. Or was there to be a closed society with closed minds?

Lee had also noticed a strange air of unreality about Parliament. It was like watching men chasing after shadows and battling with illusions. They would often pick on a trivial subject and debate it as though it were essential. All the while one truly important reality of the Malaysian situation was being avoided in parliament like the plague.

The subject was, of course, the racial problem.

It was the one compelling issue that was being discussed quietly in the streets and coffee-shops, places where people had more faith in rumours than in government-sponsored news. Clearly, it had become a forbidden topic in parliament – the one place where it needed to be discussed, debated and crystallized. Everyone knew the problem existed. But the unwritten rule determined it should be ignored in the hope it would disappear.

To Lee it seemed dangerous to cover up racial matters in this manner. He knew, only too well, how rumours thrived in unmonitored conditions and spread like infections. It seemed wiser, in his view, to bring the racial problem out into the open and examine it in a calm and healthy atmosphere, with commonsense and goodwill.

If people could see it as it really was and be shown its dangers, they would more readily accept suggested solutions.

But anyone who dared raise these matters openly had to be prepared to meet the fury of the violent men on the government back benches. He must face the risk of being shouted down and branded a trouble-maker and a traitor.

He would also be accused of being anti-Malay. Malays were *bumiputras* – sons of the soil, masters of the house. Non-Malays were *bangsa asing* – aliens, who were abusing their hospitality.

Lee spoke late into the night, but members on both sides listened intently as he continued:

"They (the Malay extremists) have triggered off something basic and fundamental. Malaysia – to whom does it belong? To Malaysians. But who are Malaysians? I hope I am, Mr Speaker, Sir. But sometimes, sitting in this chamber, I doubt whether I am allowed to be a Malaysian. This is the doubt that hangs over many minds, and the next contest, if this goes on, will be on very different lines.

"Once emotions are set in motion, and men pitted against men along these unspoken lines, you will have the kind of warfare that will split the nation from top to bottom and undo Malaysia. Everybody knows it. I don't have to say it. It is the unspoken word!"

THE 'ULTRAS'

Lee Kuan Yew spent New Year's Day 1965 in quiet reflection. The old year had ended on a wrong note with Tan Siew Sin's budget and the unseemly behaviour he was subjected to in parliamentary sessions in Kuala Lumpur. But Lee was a tenacious politician and focused his hopes instead on the leaders who were still in good heart and could help achieve the best for Malaysia. He remained hopeful and still saw a bright future. If only the extremists could be stopped and their intolerance banished!

The Singapore leader's wish for a Malaysian Malaysia took a beating in the months that followed. The intolerance increased; the racist campaign was stepped up. He saw Malaysia drifting towards disaster.

Lee had anticipated there would be teething troubles in the first few years of Malaysia's existence, a period of difficult adjustment, but he had not expected such level of hostility. It had never occurred to him the Tunku would allow the secondary leaders of UMNO unfettered liberty to push their dangerous racial agenda.

He had referred to these 'hatchet men' in that moving speech in Parliament. By the new year, he much preferred to call them the 'Ultras' or 'the mad Mullahs'.

A number of them were now controlling UMNO.

There was Syed Jaafar Albar. His name suggested an Arab ancestry. The Secretary General of UMNO was the most dangerous of them all. The Malaysian 'Who's Who' revealed he had been born in Indonesia and had come to Malaya as an adult. Yet this man could claim to be Malay and accepted as local. He could also claim a higher political status and demand more rights than a non-Malay whose family had lived in Malaysia for three generations.

Senu bin Abdul Rahman was an Albar ally. Senu was referred to in releases as the 'bald-headed youth leader' of the UMNO Youth Section. He was also Minister of Information and Broadcasting. He had started life as a Malay schoolteacher and had gone to the United States for a political science course. On his return he had 'purified' himself by immersion in the back-waters of Malay politics, the breeding ground of racial extremists.

There was Syed Nasir bin Ismail. He was the man behind the mission to force the Malay language down the willing throats of non-Malays faster than they could swallow it. He believed it was his sacred duty to restore 'the sovereignty' of the Malay language, and, through it, the sovereignty of the Malay race.

Apart from these three, there were many others less known but no less dangerous and hostile to the concept of a multi-racial Malaysia.

In the old Malaya, these men had been comfortable and secure. The Malays made up half the population of Malaya but controlled two-thirds of the seats in Parliament. The Alliance pattern of politics made them doubly secure. The UMNO, the MCA and the MIC were in separate communal compartments. The Alliance provided an attractive appearance of inter-racial harmony, but it also gave the Malays a firm guarantee of continuing control.

With Malaysia, and now, the concept of a Malaysian Malaysia, they perceived their privileged status threatened. Singapore's huge Chinese population had upset the balance. They had been made aware of new facts: The Malays now made up 39 per cent of the total population, the Chinese 42 per cent, and the others 19 per cent. If the old Alliance pattern could be maintained, and extended to the new states of Malaysia, the Malays would still have a chance. They would still be able to dominate Malaya, the biggest component, and through it the other states of Malaysia. With the submissive cooperation of the MCA, they would continue to be secure. But there was one vital factor in all this – the Malays must be kept solidly together at all costs.

UMNO leaders found themselves confronted by a formidable opponent. In Singapore, the PAP under Lee Kuan

Yew, had campaigned on a multi-racial platform in September 1963 and won Malay support away from UMNO. He promised them progress through better education and modern economic techniques. The PAP gained every Malay seat in that election.

The leaders of UMNO saw the danger in Lee's presence. If his brand of politics were to spread to Malaya, their power would be seriously undermined. The 'Ultras' decided to fight back at once and to fight harshly, bitterly. They would fight Lee's challenge not only in Malaya but in Singapore as well. They embarked on a fiery campaign of racial incitement, the roots of the Singapore riots in 1964. When the violence and bloodshed did not erode Malay support for Lee in Singapore, the 'Ultras' felt the situation demanded even more drastic action.

The Tunku's 'boys' found particularly disturbing Lee's confident prediction of a new alignment of political forces across the peninsula. As Lee was suggesting it, there would be a clear division between those seeking a Malaysian Malaysia and those sticking to a racially-divided nation with one racial grouping dominating the rest.

The 'Ultras' saw that if Lee's success was not stubbed out quickly, it would unbalance the power structure and eventually erode their control. Lee had to be stopped! But how?

One way was to change their whole approach and meet Lee on his own ground. This meant going in for multi-racial politics themselves. Another method was to put Lee away and take over Singapore. To do this they would have to fiddle with the constitution. The latter recourse was most unseemly, but, then, the 'Ultras' were capable of anything.

A battle through the homegrown press was thought most useful. They could pursue an unrelenting vitriolic campaign against the PAP leader through the pages of *Utusan Melayu*. They could reach its vast Malay readership and warn of the ambitious intruder from Singapore. They would bait the Singapore PM; they would force him to make statements which they, in turn, could manipulate and declare to be against the wider interests of Malaysia. They would make him appear hungry for power, even out to topple the Tunku. Nobody reading *Utusan Melayu* would remain unmoved by that.

Senu had already warned Singapore not to stand in proud defiance against Kuala Lumpur. A more ominous threat was made by Rahman Talib, Minister of Education. The *Utusan Melayu* had Talib saying: "The Tunku took a gamble in accepting Singapore, for as we have often said, Singapore is like a thorn in Malaysia's flesh. The time has arrived for the people of Singapore to decide whether they prefer to live under Lee Kuan Yew's rule or under the rule of Tunku Abdul Rahman. If the answer is for Lee Kuan Yew, the Central Government should reconsider Singapore's position in Malaysia."

Was it safe to ignore such threats? Lee felt it would be wiser to warn the desperate men of the consequences of acting outside the constitution: "You know the British have got hundreds of thousands of troops, but they decided that they could not hold Singapore against the wishes of the people. So slowly and very prudently, they retreated and handed over power to the elected leaders. To act contrary to the wishes of the people, contrary to what has been agreed, will make us like South Vietnam."

For good measure, Lee warned the 'Ultras' that Malaysia's allies – Britain, Australia and New Zealand – had neither the will nor the capacity for the American type of role in Vietnam.

On March 5, 1965, Lee flew to Australia and New Zealand at the invitation of their governments. In Kuala Lumpur, suspicious eyes watched him leave. This journey was to be used as further ammunition against the PAP politician.

Lee explained to his Australian and New Zealand opposite numbers that Malaysia, despite its present internal problems was still worth defending against Sukarno. It must succeed, not for itself alone but for the whole region. If it failed – either gobbled up by Sukarno or destroyed by racial strife – Australia and New Zealand would suffer!

But Lee took along another message as well. Australia and New Zealand were close and trusted friends of Malaysia and their advice was usually listened to with respect. They should now use their influence to persuade the Tunku to make Malaysia an equal and open society.

Lee was met by a large dose of skepticism within Australian left-wing circles, especially the trade unions. They were not impressed with what they had heard and observed of Malaysia so far. It seemed to be lacking in many of the basic requirements for a just and free society. The left-wing were afraid that in backing Malaysia, they would one day find themselves propping up a reactionary government.

But Lee also found in Australia and New Zealand an intelligent interest in Malaysia's racial problems. He was able to put across succinctly to a sober, thinking audience what he had been trying to explain for months on end. His enemies had tried to make out he was against giving special privileges to the Malays. This wasn't strictly true. He was not opposed to the special privileges as such, but he thought there was a better way to solve the problems of poverty.

Giving a backward peasant a gold coin would not end his troubles. It would only encourage him to demand two, and then three gold coins. A continuing dependence would only make him a lesser man. The real solution was to make him a more efficient farmer and increase his earning capacity.

The solution was education. An educated man would be in a better position to achieve his aspirations.

Lee also set out to demolish the dangerous myth that only the Malays were poor. It was true that there were many Chinese millionaires, but hundreds of thousands of Chinese and Indians were just as impoverished as many Malays. The line dividing the haves and the have-nots was not a racial one. This was an economic problem which needed an economic rather than a racial solution. But for saying this, he was being branded a dangerous trouble-maker and accused of being anti-Malay.

Lee made a substantial impact during his trip. Wherever he went Malaysian students flocked to listen to him. A news agency reported that, in Sydney alone, 500 of them gave him a 'fantastic' reception.

An American student described the scene at the University of Adelaide: "The Union theatre was overflowing. Hundreds of students were sitting on the lawn in front of the library where loudspeakers were set up. There has never been such a large crowd for a speaker."

The *Auckland Star* said Lee had performed "an invaluable service in clearing the New Zealand and Australian air of doubts about the validity of Malaysia."

From the *Christchurch Star* came this praise: "The new Malaysian Federation has an articulate and powerful advocate in the person of Lee Kuan Yew."

The *Canberra Times* was equally impressed: "Lee Kuan Yew is something of an elder statesman, though his critics sometimes try to dismiss him as a brash young man in too much of a hurry . . . he is an unrepentant Malaysian . . . a man of considerable political talent and driving industry . . . an up-and-doing politician, a pragmatist."

The *Sydney Morning Herald* trumpeted: "In Lee Kuan Yew, Australia welcomes a man who can be fairly ranked as the most able political figure in all Southeast Asia, shrewd, tough-minded and supremely a realist."

From *The Bulletin* news magazine in Australia came another ringing endorsement: ". . . Lee Kuan Yew proved himself a good ambassador for Malaysia. He goes back to Singapore, his reputation as a brilliant, tough Asian politician untarnished. Whether this will be appreciated by his fierce critics in Malaysia . . . is Mr Lee's affair."

The Bulletin's comment was most apt. The acknowlegements of Lee's brilliance made the 'Ultras' in Kuala Lumpur all the more furious. Every accolade that went Lee Kuan Yew's way sent them apoplectic. Senu bin Abdul Rahman, instructed Radio Malaysia and TV Malaysia to keep the coverage on Lee to the barest minimum. Radio Malaysia gave 30 lines in a news bulletin to a 'Crush Malaysia' speech by Sukarno, and there were no complaints. But 10 lines in the same bulletin devoted to Lee brought angry protests, even though the item showed Lee putting up a stout defence of Malaysia.

As far as the 'Ultras' were concerned, Lee had gone to Australia and New Zealand to project his own image and had succeeded too well. They even criticised the Malaysian High Commissioner in Canberra for doing nothing to counter Lee. They now demanded that an Alliance mission be sent to the two countries to undo what Lee had done.

Lee returned from his Australian tour in high spirits. On May 1, as Singapore celebrated its 'State Day', he made a forecast:

"The future is fair, and certainly not bleak," he declared. To this, he added: "Our future depends upon our collective will and endurance to forge relentlessly towards a Malaysian Malaysia."

This was the new banner. A Malaysian Malaysia. A Malaysia in which all Malaysians would be equal. A Malaysia in which economic defects would be repaired with economic tools, and not just by one racial group dominating the others.

Sunday, May 2, was a good day. From the tiny state of Perlis came a voice of sanity. The Mentri Besar of Perlis, the State's Chief Minister, Dato Sheikh Ahmad addressed himself to Lee Kuan Yew.

Sheikh Ahmad had a son studying in Australia when Lee went there. The boy was so upset over Lee's speeches that he asked his father to transfer him to London. The old man's knee jerk reaction was to join the demand for the central government to send a mission to Australia to put its own case across. He had even offered to join it.

But ten days later, Sheikh Ahmad appeared to have cooled down. Now he was appealing to Lee to forget past quarrels and make a fresh start. He said: "If there was so much goodwill and enthusiasm at the birth of Malaysia, why should there be any dissension now? Let me, therefore, say this to Mr Lee: If you will, as you say, respect the rights of the Malays, then let us all be friends. Let us shake hands and begin anew to build up national solidarity. There is no reason for Malaysians to make enemies of one another when we already have a common enemy."

But Sheikh Ahmad's words were drowned by the shrill objections of Syed Jaafar Albar. Albar said Sheikh Ahmad's appeal to Lee had shocked him. He would never trust Lee. Albar insisted: "Lee's intentions are very clear. He will use every opportunity to influence the Malays."

In Singapore, Lee welcomed Sheikh Ahmad's appeal, but he doubted if it would lead to anything. It was useless, he said, to talk of national solidarity unless the leaders in Kuala Lumpur called off their racial campaign and worked for a genuine Malaysian Malaysia.

Around this time, a story started circulating among the UMNO leadership in Kuala Lumpur about Lee's assertion that the Malays really couldn't lay claim to be more native to Malaya than the other races. The report added Lee as saying that it was wrong and illogical for a particular group to think they were more justified to be called Malaysians, and that the others can become Malaysians only through their favour.

How much was fact and how much was fiction got lost in the breast-beating emotionalism that followed.

Jaafar Albar who had arrived in Malaya from Indonesia shortly before the outbreak of World War 11 when he was past 30 years of age, sounded most adamant.

"To say that the Malays are in the same category as the other races is an insult to the Malays," he thundered. Again, he accused Lee of being anti-Malay.

Syed Nasir bin Ismail, the Malay language champion, joined Albar. "This is an unprecedented insult to the Malays who first came to Malaya about 3,000 years before Christ," he solemnly pronounced.

A more chilling warning came from the UMNO party newspaper *Malaya Merdeka.* "If Singapore's position is not reviewed and no concrete action is taken against leaders who have sown communal hatred, we cannot prophesy what will happen to our young country," an item read.

It went on: "If the Malays are hard-pressed and their interests are not protected, they will be forced to merge the country with Indonesia."

Lee was taken aback by the violence of these attacks. He found it painful to hear that some Malaysians were more Malaysian than others. "I do not know when the ancestors of the two gentlemen (Albar and Nasir) came to Malaya. One, I know, came from Indonesia. But I can trace my ancestors back to three generations, or about 100 years in Singapore," he quipped.

The Singapore PM left shortly thereafter for Bombay to attend an Asian socialist conference. His absence made his arch enemies more active. Senu bin Abdul Rahman was up in arms, complaining to an UMNO gathering that Lee had humiliated the Malays. He warned Lee that such tactics would destroy the Chinese in Malaysia.

Then came an unexpected blast from the deputy prime minister himself. In a blunt statement to the press, Tun Abdul Razak told Singapore that if it wished to work together with the rest of Malaysia, it must find another leader who was sincere.

Syed Jaafar Albar inspecting the "crush Lee Kuan Yew" placards carried by UMNO party faithful during a political gathering in Kuala Lumpur in May, 1965.

"Mr Lee has upset not only the Malay people but also the Malay rulers and everybody else," Tun Razak remarked. The mention of the Malay rulers gave the affair an added dimension, a precarious one that made the bitter altercation go beyond normal politics into extremely dangerous territory. The statement could be read as a call to prove loyalty to the sultans by rising and defending their race, religion and country.

Placards denouncing Lee and demanding his arrest now added colour to UMNO meetings called by the 'Ultras'. In one gathering, the rabble-rousing ended in the burning of Lee's effigy.

The row escalated while the Tunku was in Tokyo. When he returned home ten days later, a reporter asked him, during a stopover in Hong Kong, if Lee had any chance of becoming prime minister of Malaysia. "I wish him luck," the Tunku replied. "I am a tired man. If he can succeed, let him take over. But I don't think our people are ready to surrender power to him."

The storm gathered fury. Lee was the main topic at the UMNO annual assembly attended by more than a thousand delegates in mid-May. Another denunciation of Lee was orchestrated and nobody tried to tackle these latest provocations. More placards demanding Lee be crushed were displayed by members of the party faithful. If Lee couldn't be crushed, then he could at least be arrested.

The Tunku advised his angry supporters to hold their fire. He called for unity. He told UMNO men: "It is obvious every right thinking person feels that Singapore's place is with Malaysia. Without Malaya, Singapore would not enjoy the prosperity she is enjoying today."

But the Alliance leader did not censure those behind the placards that called for either the crushing or the arrest of Lee.

Lee followed these disheartening developments from Bangkok on his way to Cambodia from Laos. He was glad no one was going to do anything as stupid as trying to arrest him. "If you arrest a man for differences of opinion, what do you do next?" he asked.

THE UNBENDING BACKBONE

Lee returned from his Asian tour on May 21, 1965, determined not to yield to the growing pressures against him. He went on TV Singapore to warn the people that there were men in high positions in UMNO who resisted a Malaysian Malaysia and would prefer to use unconstitutional methods to make sure of it. On this fundamental issue, he said, he could never give way.

"If people do not want a Malaysian Malaysia through constitutional methods, let us know now," Lee declared. "We can make alternative arrangements. It is no use making sacrifices for the defence of Malaysia against Indonesian confrontation if it is not to be a Malaysian Malaysia."

The pressure kept mounting. The *Utusan Melayu* kept churning out its Albar-inspired propaganda day after day in bigger and stronger doses. Its headlines screamed fierce threats from Albar and the other 'Ultras'.

On May 23, Albar addressed a Malay gathering in Peninsular Malaya. This meeting was reported in the *Utusan Melayu* under the headline: ALBAR CHALLENGES LEE KUAN YEW.

Albar said: "If Lee is a man he should not twist and turn. He should be brave enough to say 'I want to leave Malaysia because I am no longer satisfied with it.'" Raising his voice, Albar asked: "What about it?" The crowd replied: 'Crush Lee, crush Lee.' Dropping his voice, Albar said: "Undoubtedly Lee is like the 'sepat' fish which lives in muddy water." Several voices responded: 'Catch Lee and pickle him.' Albar smiled and replied: "Shout louder so that Dr Ismail can hear the anger of the people."

Albar was incensed that the Minister of Internal Security would not agree to have Lee arrested. It was Dr Ismail's view that Lee had not breached the law and the differences he had with the leadership of UMNO must be fought within the law, constitutionally. This left the UMNO secretary general angrier.

On May 24, Albar addressed another gathering and told his Malay audience that in meeting the challenge before them they must unite more closely and realise their identity. "Wherever I am, I am a Malay," he declared.

Lee read these reports with increasing concern and voiced his feelings in parliament. "If I had been going round and saying what the member for Johore Tenggara has been saying – wherever I am, I am a Chinese – where would we be? But I keep on reminding the people that I am a Malaysian. I am learning *Bahasa Kebangsaan* and I accept article 153 of the Constitution." The article covers the special position and rights of the Malays and the indigenous people of Sabah and Sarawak.

How much better for Malaysia, he remarked later, if Albar had said: 'Wherever I am, I am a Malaysian.' The pot was being brought steadily to the boil. Lee explained to some of his supporters in Singapore that there was a clear reason why this was being done. If bones are boiled long enough they melt into glue. The 'Ultras' were deliberately turning on the heat against the non-Malays in the hope that their backbones would melt and they would become as spineless as the leaders of the MCA.

The dividing line between the political forces began to be drawn more clearly as Lee had predicted. In a bid to have a stronger voice, the leaders of five opposition parties had got together in May, 1965, to form the Malaysian Solidarity Convention (MSC). Its aim: to achieve a Malaysian Malaysia through peaceful and constitutional means. There was no doubt its prime mover was Lee himself. He explained the MSC was not interested in opposing anyone: "We want to establish, not a new government, but acceptance of the fundamental principle written in the Constitution that we are all Malaysians regardless of race, creed or colour."

UMNO leaders remained hostile. To them, Lee had roped in the other opposition parties to widen his attack on the special position of the Malays. The Tunku now warned the people to beware of Lee. Emboldened by this, Albar lashed out again, demanding once more immediate action against Lee before it was too late. "This man must not be allowed to go any further in his attempt to destroy Malaysia," he stated.

Listening to it all, Lee remembered the lessons he had learned fighting the communists in Singapore."We were brought up in the hardest school of all, and we learned how to deal with tough guys. Utter and absolute stamina and perseverance," he declared. In this spirit of defiance he attended the next meeting of the Malaysian Parliament. The leaders of the MSC had held a special meeting among themselves to work out a common strategy. The scene was set for a spectacular clash.

The opening of the new session of parliament on May 25 was a glittering affair: a military parade, a fanfare of trumpets, guns booming out in salute, the men with their medals, the women in their elegant finery. The King, in royal Malay costume, was present, sitting on the throne, the Queen beside him. The Tunku bowed and presented the Royal Address to His Majesty which the Agong read to the assembly. The speech lasted 35 minutes. In substance it centred on how Malaysia had forged ahead in spite of difficult problems. It included praise for the Tunku's outstanding leadership.

The Royal Address ended with a warning. "We are now facing threats to our security from Indonesia. In addition, we are also facing threats from within the country. Both these threats are designed to create trouble. If those concerned achieve their objective, it will mean chaos for us and an end to democracy."

An up-and-coming UMNO backbencher, Dr Mahathir Mohamad, was given the honour of proposing a motion of thanks to His Majesty. After a hurried 'Thank You' to the King, the young doctor from Kedah swung into a bitter racial attack on Lee and his followers. The vehemence was shocking. Mahathir said the Chinese in Singapore who supported Lee were selfish and arrogant, living in a purely Chinese environment where Malays could only exist as chauffeurs. The Chinese lived in palaces, went about in huge cars and had the best things in life, while the so-called 'privileged' lived in huts.

"They have never known Malay rule and cannot bear the idea that the people they have so long kept under their heels should now be in a position to rule them," the UMNO politician asserted. He said Lee wanted to be the first Chinese prime minister of Malaysia, and was even willing to see Malaysia destroyed to achieve his mad ambition.

"The PAP objects to a Malay capitalist class but works very hard to create an all-powerful Chinese capitalist class so that Chinese hegemony in the economic field can be perpetuated," he went on. "This, of course, would be an advantage to a Chinese political party."

The Malaysian Parliament had never heard anything like this before. To D.R.Seenivasagam of the MSC, it was unprecedented. He called Mahathir 'a chauvinist of the first grade'. He wondered how men like Mahathir and Albar were free to roam around the country inciting racial trouble.

Dr Lim Chong Eu, also of the MSC, was dismayed. It was such a pity that the debate on the King's speech should have been used to inflame racial passions. He said: "This is a sad day but we have to accept the challenge because it involves deep-seated emotional issues and constitutional matters."

Lee Kuan Yew had felt the sting of the warning at the end of the King's address. The day following Mahathir's spirited attack on the PAP, he voiced disappointment that nothing about a continuing goal for a Malaysian Malaysia was included in the Royal Address and proposed an amendment to express this. He was also anxious to have a point clarified and he requested the Tunku to answer it. Who were the enemies within? Lee asked pointedly: "Is it perhaps we – loyal Malaysians gathering to establish a Malaysian Malaysia – who are the threat from within?"

An UMNO backbencher shouted back: "Yes, it is the PAP."

Tun Abdul Razak dismissed Lee's question with a curt reply. The King, he explained, had been referring to the communists. Elaborating, Tun Razak said: "As the Chief Executive of Singapore with the information at his disposal, Mr Lee knew full well that the enemies within were the communists."

Lee chose to play down the matter during the five-day debate but he also delivered another splendid speech, this time partly in the Malay language.

What had he done to be branded an enemy of the country? He believed in a Malaysian Malaysia, and he honoured the constitution because that was what he had sworn to do. Listening to

Mahathir's remarks about Malay rule, it was clear to him that the 'Ultras' in UMNO did not want a Malaysia in which all Malaysians would be equal. They wanted a Malay Malaysia. With such men around, it would probably take ten years to establish a Malaysian Malaysia, but he would stick it out.

For weeks, he said, the 'Ultras' had been accusing him of wanting to take Singapore out of Malaysia. Sorry – but he could not oblige them. His friends and he would not leave and abandon Malaysia to the tender mercies of racists like Albar. "We tell him and all his colleagues now – we have not the slightest intention of seceding," Lee advised.

There was no question of getting out of Malaysia. It was also important to expose the fallacy that all Chinese were fat and rich. The truth was that less than one per cent of the Chinese in Singapore were rich businessmen. Trying to turn one per cent of the Malays into rich capitalists while ignoring the rest would never solve the problem of Malay poverty.

In the end, Lee pursued, the political contest would have to be decided on the real issues, like providing better housing, health and education, and raising the earning capacity of the people. Those with superior techniques should be free to sell them to the people. They should not be silenced with threats of violence.

"All right, stifle us," the Singapore leader continued. "Shut down the volume and take over the radio station. We will keep quiet? No. The voice will be heard ultimately. It will echo in the hearts and minds of the people."

His amendment to the motion of thanks to the King was not meant as disrespect, he explained. He was merely taking advantage of a parliamentary device. He had wanted the motion to express regret that the Royal Address had not reassured the nation that Malaysia would become a Malaysian Malaysia. He also wanted it to say that, to the contrary, doubts had been created as to the intentions of the government.

Dr Ismail countered by claiming it was the PAP leader who was destroying Malaysia's racial harmony and blaming UMNO for it.

Senu bin Abdul Rahman came next. He dug out a statement Lee was reported to have made in Australia, attacking the Tunku's leadership. Lee had denied it in Australia itself, and anyone reading could see that it was a garbled report. Among other distortions, the report quoted Lee as saying: "Yes, my father is an Indonesian."

But Senu insisted on using the report. When Lee tried to object, there was uproar from the government benches. His protest was drowned in shouts of "shut up ... sit down ... traitor get out!"

The Speaker banged his gavel for order and Senu continued his attack.

Lee went back to Singapore over the weekend and spoke at a small function. He referred to Mahathir's speech in parliament and said Singapore had never agreed to Malay rule. It wanted Malaysian rule. If there were other people who were determined to have Malay rule, alternative arrangements would have to be made, and the sooner the better. Those states which wanted a Malaysian Malaysia could get together.

The local English language newspaper, *The Straits Times*, reported Lee's speech under the headline –

LEE GIVES A HINT: IT COULD BE PARTITION.

Lee was quick to point out he had not used the word partition and had not meant it. But nobody in Kuala Lumpur would listen. It was too late. The damage had been done and UMNO was determined to run with it.

Tun Razak, got his teeth into the issue and refused to let go. At the end of the five-day debate in parliament, he asserted that Lee's latest pronouncements had made the "gulf between the People's Action Party and the Alliance now wide and clear." The PAP, Tun Razak said derisively, clearly stood for '*Partition and Perish*'. In Malay that was *Pechah dan Punah*.

Lee tried desperately to intervene, to explain that he had not said or meant partition, to point out that the first person to talk about partition had been none other than the Tunku himself as far back as December 9, 1964. On that occasion the Tunku had said: "If the politicians of various colours, tinges and flashes in Singapore disagree with me, the only solution is a breakaway, but what a calamity that would be for Singapore and Malaysia." Lee tried to draw attention to this statement. His words were again interrupted by jeers and shouts. It was impossible.

In the end, the vote on Mahathir's motion of thanks to the King was taken and passed to thunderous applause. But the session ended on an extremely uncertain note with the future of Malaysia in the balance.

For the next few weeks, Lee watched a more concerted propaganda exercise get mounted against him personally and the PAP in general. The central government mobilized every tool it had under its command. The press warned the people that Lee Kuan Yew was trying to break up Malaysia. TV Malaysia in Kuala Lumpur presented a forum every night called 'Partition and Perish'. All the speakers were Alliance supporters and they were unanimous in their conclusion that Lee was a dangerous man.

Lee was not cowed by all this. He said his experiences over a decade had taught him one important thing – ". . . that only those count and matter who have the strength and courage of their convictions to stick up and stand for what they believe in, for their people, for their country, regardless of what happens to themselves."

Smiles belie true feelings. Lee Kuan Yew and visiting Malaysian Finance Minister Tan Siew Sin meet on the evening of June 25, 1964, at a dinner hosted by the four Chambers of Commerce in Singapore.

A relaxed Tunku in August, 1964, shares a dinner-time joke with PAP leaders at Singapore's St. Patrick's school. The occasion marked the end of a two-day tour of the island by the Malaysian leader who, together with Lee Kuan Yew, visited areas considered most sensitive during the previous month's rioting. The dinner was hosted by goodwill committees of the 51 local constituencies. This photograph shows Lee seated to the Tunku's right and Minister of National Development Lim Kim San on his left. Standing to the rear is Singapore's Finance Minister Goh Keng Swee.

SECTION 3

Tan Siew Sin, heir to huge financial wealth and formidable family political connections, sought to preserve, at all costs, a political status quo. A substantial part of this section deals with the impact Tan, President of the Malayan Chinese Association (MCA), had on the merger and separation issues and renders his side of the story.

The Man from Malacca

Confronting Lee Kuan Yew

Dealing with the Wreckers

The Fight Goes on

A to Z and Z to A

The Josey Affair

Destination Disaster

The Final Act

Malacca's beloved son and founding president of the Malayan Chinese Association (MCA) – Tun Dato Sir Tan Cheng Lock, father of Tan Siew Sin.

Representing the Malayan government's Chinese viewpoint, MCA President Tan Cheng Lock (far right) participates in the historic Baling peace talks in December, 1955.

THE MAN FROM MALACCA

At the end of June 1965, while the Tunku lay ill in London, reflecting on the problems back home and Lee Kuan Yew in Singapore brooded about the future of Malaysia, a third man in Kuala Lumpur was likewise pondering where the events of the past months would finally lead. Tan Siew Sin, Minister of Finance in Malaysia and President of the MCA, was filled with anxiety and gloom. He had come to the conclusion that Lee Kuan Yew was the most disruptive force in Malaysia.

No two men could have been more unlike each other. While Lee boasted peasant antecedents, Tan was born to great wealth. Tan had the effete ways of the old rich; Lee displayed the brashness of a self-made man.

Tan's great-grandfather left a considerable estate to which his great-grandson became an executor and beneficiary. This inheritance was expanded by the business acumen of Siew Sin's father, Dato Sir Tan Cheng Lock. He trained his son how to handle business and, through cautious ways, to retain wealth. Siew Sin proved an astute learner. He enlarged further on his great-grand-father's and father's legacies. Despite this vast fortune, Tan Siew Sin was famous throughout both his political and business careers for frugality and his unostentatious way of living. He demanded style, but that did not necessarily mean extravagance or flamboyance. This was how fellow politicians and his own family would remember him.

In later skirmishes with Lee, Tan Siew Sin would volunteer that he did not have to touch his great-grandfather's bequest.

As one of its executors, he deemed it fit to distribute monthly allowances to needy relations from the proceeds of investments left in the old man's will.

Tan had grown up in Malacca, once the seat of an ancient Malay empire and a great trading centre. Four hundred and fifty years of colonial rule by the Portuguese, the Dutch and eventually the British had reduced it to the sleepy hollow of Malaysia. In the meantime, Lee Kuan Yew's Singapore, infused with Chinese talent and energy and occupying a more strategic geographical position, had risen to replace Malacca as the region's thriving, bustling business centre.

There were two achievements of which the Malacca Chinese were particularly proud. In Malacca, more than anywhere else in Malaysia, the Chinese had learned to live on the closest possible terms with the Malays. Over the years they had imbibed a good deal of Malay culture. Many had even forgotten their own mother-tongue and spoke a crude form of Malay. Their food, dress sense and dances showed strong traces of Malay influence.

The second pride of the Malacca Chinese was a leader who had sprung up from their midst. He was Tan Cheng Lock, father of Tan Siew Sin. Since the 1920s, he had dreamed and spoken about an independent Malaya in which the Chinese would have an equal place with the Malays.

Tan Cheng Lock voiced these sentiments when he observed: "The combination of different races in one state is as necessary a condition of civilised life as the combination of men in society. Inferior races are raised by living in political union with races intellectually superior. Exhausted and decaying races are revived by the contact of a younger vitality.

"A state which is incompetent to satisfy different races condemns itself. A state which labours to neutralise, to absorb, or to expel them, destroys its own vitality. A state which does not include them is destitute of the chief basis of self-government. Practically every state in the modern world is multi-national... Cultural diversity is as desirable as individual diversity. Variety is the indispensable condition of the advance of the human mind."

But the British – the ruling colonial power – had opposed Tan Cheng Lock from the beginning and had insisted on giving the Malays a special, privileged position, while treating the Chinese

Sir Hugh Charles Clifford, Governor of the Straits Settlements from June, 1927, until February, 1930. It was Sir Hugh who urged Britain to be always mindful of her 'duty' to help the Malays 'rule their own country.'

as aliens. Sir Hugh Clifford, a famous British High Commissioner, had once said: "Let everyone in this country be mindful of the fact that this is a Malay country, and we British came here at the invitation of Their Highnesses the Malay Rulers, and it is our duty to help the Malays to rule their own country."

There were obviously many who did not subscribe to this idea and for one brief period after the war, it had seemed the British, too, had changed their minds. But they quickly yielded to Malay pressure and went back to the old pattern, to the disappointment of the non-Malays.

The discontent that followed made the internal situation in the peninsula ripe for revolt as far as the communists were concerned.

In June, 1948, the CPM launched its bloody insurrection that was to last twelve long years. Among the first victims of the Malayan Emergency were large sections of the Chinese community. They were harassed and persecuted under harsh 'Emergency Regulations' imposed by the British, simply because most of the communists were Chinese. Thousands of Chinese were banished to an unknown fate in China on the flimsiest suspicions. It didn't matter whether the 'banishees' had ever been to China or not.

By this time the Malays had already banded solidly together under the banner of UMNO to resist the earlier British attempt to interfere with their special rights. The Chinese had no such political organisation to represent them and Tan Cheng Lock stepped forward to fill the vacuum, setting up the MCA. The British may have encouraged him to do this, for they knew that such a party could be an effective weapon against the communists. Still, it was Tan Cheng Lock who supplied the courage and the hard work for this task. It needed a lot of guts at the time. The CPM, too, saw that the MCA could become a dangerous rival and set out to destroy it in its infancy.

The MCA expanded rapidly and within eight months its membership rose to over one hundred thousand. It organised a massive welfare service for Chinese victims of the Emergency, and paid for it with money from a country-wide lottery. This lottery eventually became so successful that the government decided to take it over and runs it to this day.

Within a few years, the British began to see that the Emergency was not a simple military struggle. It was far more complex. If the people were to be prevented from going over to the communists, Malaya had to be given something worthwhile to look forward to and fight for. The frequently repeated colonial phrase – 'a battle for the hearts and minds of the people' – happened to reflect a large measure of truth.

Victory in this battle meant independence. *Merdeka.*

But independence was not an easy solution. The British realised the many complications in the Malayan situation. If handled the wrong way, independence could destroy Malaya.

The Chinese were very apprehensive about their future. What would happen to them after the British left? It was true that they were immigrants, or the children and grandchildren of immigrants. But, they had worked harder than anyone else to build modern Malaya. Many had perished in the struggle, killed in the general lawlessness of the early pioneering days or destroyed by malaria by courtesy of the devilish anopheles mosquito. The Chinese felt they, too, were Malayans, and equally so.

The problem seemed enormous and the fears too real until the Alliance Party came along. Even then, its inception was met with forebodings. How could erstwhile rivals, UMNO and MCA, work together? How could they be partners when the primary function of each was to protect its members against the other? The experiment was surely bound to fail.

To everyone's astonishment the Alliance became an immediate success. It worked because it introduced a new pattern of approach into Malayan politics. It enabled the Malays, the Chinese and the Indians to maintain their own racial political parties, while their leaders began to work more closely together. They met regularly to settle mutual problems, work out common policies and arrange for their parties to cooperate whenever necessary. This was essentially a process of bargaining among the leaders for concessions from one another.

It also meant that all the major delicate issues affecting the Malays and the non-Malays had to be put in the chiller and could be discussed only by men at the top, quietly, with infinite patience and tact, in the secrecy of private chambers. Under no circumstances must any of the partners take a public stand on any racial issue until full agreement had been reached. Keen public discussions had to be discouraged for they could easily create tension and ill will.

This, of course, took the fun and excitement out of politics. It starved the Alliance politician of the stuff a politician normally thrives upon. He must forget the headlines except in such safe issues as communism and colonialism. No longer could he pose as the champion of some oppressed group, especially if it also happened to be a racial group. He must always preach, to the point of utter boredom, the message of goodwill, understanding and tolerance. He must always try to find excuses for grievances which cried out for redress. Whatever remedies there might be would have to be worked out later, in some back room.

This came to be known as the Alliance Way, based upon the belief that when men of goodwill meet, difficulties vanish. In a way it worked. It helped find solutions to many difficult problems that, otherwise, would have created upheavals. It helped to pave the way for early independence.

Occasionally some irresponsible politician ignored the agreed system and shot his mouth off, causing a minor panic. The leaders always acted swiftly to defuse such situations. The offending person was usually admonished harshly by his own party, and everything would soon be well again.

In the first general election in 1955, the Chinese and Indians had only 15 per cent of the one-and-a-quarter million votes. Had they gone it alone, the Malays could easily have won 50 of the 52 constituencies. But the Malay leaders in the Alliance gave 15 seats to the Chinese and two to the Indians. The Alliance won 51 of the 52 seats, with Malay electors voting in all the Chinese and Indian candidates.

The British made it evident that early independence could be achieved only if the Chinese continued to work closely with the Malays. Any other way could have led to acrimony and trouble, even bloodshed, and given the British an excuse for staying on. Chinese support was vital, but the Chinese were still unhappy over the fact that less than one-tenth of them were citizens. They agreed to back the drive for independence only if the citizenship laws were made more liberal. The Malay leaders in the Alliance agreed to this, in exchange for a promise from the Chinese leaders that they would support measures to help improve the economic position of the Malays. In 1957, under an independent Malaya, a million new citizens were created, 80 per cent of them Chinese. Eight years on, the gratitude had not lost its sheen.

It was Tan Siew Sin's conviction that only the Alliance could have earned the citizenships for his fellow Chinese in 1957. Malaya's progress had confounded all the prophets of doom. Independence had brought happiness and progress. Visitors from all over the world were invariably astounded to find a picture of almost blissful harmony. The country was booming and making great strides in economic and social progress. In six years of independence the national budget had expanded by more than 50 per cent and most of the extra money was being spent on infrastructure – schools, hospitals, roads, bridges. One of the happiest sights of any Malayan morning was the vast number of children going to school, children of all races in a great variety of school uniforms of different designs and colours. They made up one-fifth of the total population.

This cheerful picture was marred in 1959 when a number of 'young bloods' in the MCA began to feel that their party was being pushed around a little too much by UMNO. They decided to force a showdown, saying the Chinese were no longer willing to kowtow to the Malays. Dangerous talk this, and the Malays began to bristle. With elections round the corner, the situation took an ugly turn.

As MCA president, Tan saw his duty clearly. The harmony within the Alliance must be preserved, even though it meant that some of his stalwarts would have to leave to placate UMNO. It was a pity, for many of them were idealistic young men and some of their grievances were well-founded. Unfortunately, they had chosen to challenge UMNO publicly, violating the agreement reached among its leaders. Losing them was a heavy price to pay, but it had to be paid for the sake of peace. The damage was soon repaired, harmony was restored and the Alliance went on to win the General Election in 1959 in its usual convincing manner – 74 out of 104 seats.

When the Malaysia concept was being hatched, Tan Siew Sin promptly identified a problem. Over 75 per cent of Singapore's population was Chinese, making it 'a Chinese island'. For this reason, Singapore could afford to be much less concerned about racial issues than Malaya. Freed from such restraints, the island's politics had developed into a boisterous affair, with endless verbal brawls. The biggest brawler of them all, in Tan's view, was Lee Kuan Yew. Lee loved a fight and never hesitated to give offence. That was probably fine in Britain where he had spent his student days but in Malaya he would be the spark in a gas-filled room! Could he learn in time?

In the lead-up to Malaysia, Tan's thoughts ran thus: if only the Chinese in Singapore could be brought within the Alliance framework, this problem would be solved. The island would then be able to merge with Malaya without the slightest friction. Tan believed he could do this and set out to try. Standing in his way, though, was Lee Kuan Yew, determined to yield nothing to the MCA. Lee had even mobilized for battle the radio, television and other instruments of his state government.

By June, 1965, Tan Siew Sin was convinced he had been right about Lee all along. With the determination of a slighted aristocrat, he decided Malaysia must have no more of this pugnacious, pedantic politician. Lee Kuan Yew was better out of Malaysia. Cut him out.

CONFRONTING LEE KUAN YEW

Singapore was a paradox in the 1960s. It was a promising business hub that exuded an air of new affluence. But its character was far from committed *nouveaux riche*. The island also displayed a tense, angry side to it that manifested in constant and acrimonious industrial disputes.

Despite the strikes and the chronic labour unrest, Singapore could be proud of its achievements thus far. When Stamford Raffles arrived on the island in 1819, it was no more than a marshland inhabited by 220 Malays and a handful of Chinese. But Raffles saw its commercial potential. Geographically, the place stood at one of the vital crossroads of the world. It had the makings of an important port.

Raffles's foresight started the island's march to gradual prosperity. Under British rule, thousands of Chinese immigrants flowed into Singapore to convert its swamps into a buzzing city boasting the world's fifth largest port.

By the 1950s, Singapore was home to one and three quarter million people. The hard-working, ambitious migrants who had come in search of better lives took on new challenges and proved more than enterprising. The island possessed no natural resources. The soil was indifferent. The people realised that if they had restricted themselves to the shortcomings of their new environment, they would remain keepers of tiny vegetable gardens and small pig or poultry farms.

The migrants had to learn the business of trading and soon the island became a haven for merchants and middlemen. Singaporeans successfully built up a complex and highly efficient market-place which lived by the proud motto, 'You name it – we have it'. Into the Singapore market-place flowed the produce of neighbouring territories – rubber, tin, petroleum, pepper, copra and forest products – to be processed, packed and shipped around the world. Into it also came the world's manufactured goods from Britain, Europe and the United States, for distribution to the developing countries of Asia.

Singapore made a handsome profit from all this trading, wheeling and dealing. Malaya was Singapore's main 'hinterland'. Many Singaporeans had families and large investments in Malaya from which they derived good returns.

So, where did Singapore get its taste for left-wing politics?

It could be from all the wheeling and dealing that happened daily and the accompanying exploitation that came with unsophisticated business approaches tailored along feudal lines. Whatever its source, a number of Singaporeans acquired a taste for fierce left-wing politics.

In politics, as in trade, the Singaporeans proved robust, go-ahead men who thrived on challenge. They sneered at the genteel, old-fashioned game of politics played in 1950s Malaya by Chinese millionaires and Malay royalty. To them, the Chinese in Malaya seemed a docile and inferior breed who enjoyed being pushed around. Tan Siew Sin, MCA president, deserved nothing but contempt. In adapting to a Malay environment, he had even forgotten his own mother-tongue!

There were left-wing politicians in Singapore like Lee Kuan Yew, of the Fabian Society variety, but there were also other politicians who believed that Moscow or Peking was the fountain of all knowledge and inspiration.

Tan Siew Sin saw the formidable challenge posed by Singapore's merger with Malaya but he initially consoled himself with his belief in the innate pragmatism of the Chinese businessmen. Whatever else he might be, the Chinese was basically a hard-headed practical sort who knew where his best interests lay. He would see that smooth, friendly relations between Singapore and Kuala Lumpur would be more profitable to him than friction and hostility. The MCA could promise this better than anyone else.

But his optimism was short-lived. The Chinese in Singapore spurned Tan completely. In the 1963 Singapore state election, not a single MCA candidate was elected and most of them even lost their deposits. What was more, the voting results showed that even those who opposed Lee were not prepared to support Tan.

Tan retreated to the security of Malaya where the MCA still had the backing of the Chinese. At least there the Chinese had not forgotten it was the MCA which had helped them in the dark days of the Emergency, saved them from wholesale banishment and won them citizenship rights. There were times when they might feel that the MCA was too submissive to the Malays, but they realised that the party was still better than the communist-penetrated Socialist Front. The heartaches that one communist insurrection had caused them were more than enough for a lifetime. They could not risk another, certainly not at a time when the communists were supposedly supporting Sukarno.

If anyone doubted Tan's following in Malaya, he had only to examine the results of the 1963 Malayan local council elections. Once again, the Malayan Chinese had demonstrated their continuing gratitude and faith in the MCA by voting solidly for the Alliance. No less than three-quarters of all the seats – about 1,800 out of 2,400 – had been won by the Alliance, most of them by MCA men on Chinese votes. They had lost ground in a few towns but even there the MCA candidates had received not less than 40 per cent of the votes. Malaya was the MCA's home ground and the PAP would be crazy to challenge it there.

Like the Tunku, Tan was shocked when the PAP decided to enter the 1964 General Election in Malaya. He was also flummoxed by Lee's explanation to the Tunku. Tan found Lee's election approach most alarming, based on racial politics in a new and subtle disguise. He found most distasteful Lee's assertion that the Singapore victory had proved the urban voter now appeared ready for a grouping like the PAP. On this basis the PAP would address itself to the urban communities of Malaya while the Tunku's UMNO could look after the voters in the rural areas.

Tan read a deleterious plot in Lee's reasoning. When the PAP strongman talked of addressing urban voters, he was clearly thinking of the Chinese, and when he talked of the UMNO looking after the rural vote, he obviously meant the Malay communities. The most worrisome part of all this, from Tan's viewpoint, was that Lee appealed for Chinese support by challenging the special status of the Malays. Wasn't the Singaporean politician fully aware this was the most dangerous issue of all? If there was anything for which Malays would fight to the death, it was for their special position in Malaysian society. To top it all, while undermining everything the Tunku stood for, Lee was at the same time luring the UMNO leader to abandon the MCA and form a new alliance with the PAP.

Tan warned the Tunku that making a deal with Lee Kuan Yew would be playing with fire because of Lee's "extraordinary capacity for ditching friends." He reminded the Tunku that this was the man who had already told a Chinese audience that the Tunku lacked the calibre to lead the nation, never mind that Lee had denied ever saying it.

At a 1964 election rally, the MCA president cautioned the Malays. "We know the communists but we do not know the PAP," he told them. "They may be for you one day but there is no guarantee that they will not stab you in the back the next. If one examines their past record coldly and carefully, one cannot escape the conclusion that it is far safer to be their enemy than their friend."

Tan said Lee Kuan Yew behaved as though he had beaten the communists in Singapore single-handedly. He was not prepared to acknowledge the time when he had approached the Tunku in all humility for support. This, Tan told the crowd, was typical of Lee's arrogance.

"He tramples on those underneath him but licks the boots of those above him," he declared.

The MCA president got more alarmed when he received a report of a new and dangerous twist Lee had introduced to his election arguments. Lee, it was claimed, was saying that growing discontent with the Alliance was driving urban voters into the arms of the communists and that only the policies of the PAP could save them. If the worst transpired, the urban areas of Malaysia would eventually have to be governed like Saigon – 'with guns and bayonets!'

Tan pounced on this as further evidence that Lee was pushing a cunningly disguised racial line. In picturing an eventual struggle between the rural and urban areas, he was clearly predicting a clash between the rural Malays and the urban Chinese. Tan was now absolutely convinced Lee had been gunning for the special status of the Malays. He decided the time had come for him to speak up frankly.

On April 17, 1964, Tan went on radio to speak to the Chinese as 'one Malaysian Chinese to another'. He explained to them why he thought they were in a critical position. He said most Malays were quite liberal and supported a multi-racial Malaysia, independent and separate from Indonesia. But there was still an extremist faction that claimed the Malay race could survive only by merging with Indonesia. If the Chinese voted in a way that frightened the Malays, many of these liberals would go over to the extremists and seek merger with Sukarno's people. That would place the Chinese in a very grave position.

The warning was heeded. The election results announced on April 25 reflected Tan Siew Sin was still the undisputed leader of the Chinese in the Malayan peninsula. Twenty-seven, out of 34 MCA contenders won seats in parliament. The Socialist Front won two seats. The PAP fared even worse, limping in with a single victory.

Two bitterly opposed politicians – Singapore's S. Rajaratnam (left) and Malaysia's Dr Ismail. While both supported their separate causes with frequent, hard-hitting pronouncements there could be no mistaking each displayed considerable style.

DEALING WITH THE WRECKERS

Tan Siew Sin fervently believed that one of the miracles of modern Malaya was the racial harmony it had achieved against impossible odds. He accepted it was not the harmony of siblings, founded on affection. Rather he saw it as the understanding arrived at mutually by rivals who had the wisdom to recognise that allowing the issue of their separateness to dominate their association could yield only dire results.

The Chinese, with the confidence of over three thousand years of culture, were inclined to look down on the Malays. Rugged immigrants from a harsh land, they placed their faith in hard work and education and found success.

The Malays, fun-loving people of a generous climate, went along at a more leisurely pace and earned fewer rewards. Muslim to a man, they found their greatest strength in their religion that bound them together in suspicion and resentment of the vigorous 'kaffirs' from abroad.

In this situation, there were many points on which the Malays and the Chinese could come into conflict. And, yet, there was Lee Kuan Yew from Singapore rocking the boat, using all his political skills to underline differences which they, in old Malaya, had positioned accordingly to achieve an even keel.

What was the point of reminding the Malays they now made up only 39 per cent of the population of Malaysia? Outnumbered in their own land. Sixty-one per cent were non-Malays. Lee was really going too far. The constant harping on these figures appeared to be a deliberate move to frighten the Malays.

Tan Siew Sin warned Lee to tread carefully and avoid stepping on tender corns. It was obvious, he said, that Lee wanted power, but any party that hoped to form the Central Government of Malaysia must have the trust of the Malays and the Chinese, of both communities. Tan said the operative word was 'both'. You do not beget trust by clever talk. Something more is required and that is the people's assessment of what you are likely to do once you reach the highest seat of power. If you pass that test, you are all right. If you do not pass that test, nothing else can take its place.

From Singapore came the sound of mocking laughter. Singapore's Minister for Culture S. Rajaratnam described Tan as 'our baffled Socrates from the MCA'. He claimed Tan's vanity had been wounded by the fact that Lee Kuan Yew now commanded more respect and attention among the people of Malaysia than Tan could ever hope for. It was easy to ride a charger and be a hero, but the fact was that for many years Tan Siew Sin had found himself trapped in an extremely delicate situation. The Malays were prepared to trust him mainly because they believed, with his Malacca background, he was less Chinese than most other Chinese. They respected him for not being able to speak his mother-tongue. To them, this was proof he had broken off all ties with China and was completely loyal to Malaysia. And yet Tan was painfully aware that if he was to have any chance of winning the confidence and support of the Chinese, he must show them that he was every bit as Chinese as Lee Kuan Yew.

It was not getting easier for the man from Malacca. There were frequent complaints from members of the MCA. In the years leading up to independence the Malays had been cautious and restrained, almost apologetic, in setting out their claims to special privileges. This had changed since independence. Wherever the Chinese now turned, they were confronted with growing Malay power. Every key position in the government was filled by Malays who openly favoured their own people. Jobs, licences, land – more and more of these were being granted on racial grounds rather than merit. Malay demands for more rights and privileges were regarded as expressions of nationalism while Chinese requests for equality were immediately branded as a dangerous form of chauvinism.

The problems of leadership for a man in Tan's position were extremely trying. All he could do was advise the Chinese to be patient, pointing out to them that in spite of all the discrimination they were complaining about they were still far better off than the Chinese in Indonesia or Thailand or the Philippines. "This country has been a haven of peace and opportunity for the Chinese," he stressed. He advised them to remember that they were a mature people. They could always fall back on centuries of accumulated wisdom, confident in the knowledge that there were many fields in which no one could replace or surpass them. For this reason the Chinese had a duty to be tolerant and understanding. The Malays were a much younger race. They could be generous friends; but they could also be excitable and impetuous.

In July 1964, three months after the General Election in Malaya, the Malays in Singapore became angry, very angry. Riots exploded in the city and innocent people were killed by mobs inflamed by racial passions. This, in Tan's opinion, was the bitter fruit of Lee Kuan Yew's campaign. Such riots were dangerous even in Singapore – a small, compact island that could be easily policed. It was terrifying to think of what could happen if such racial riots spread to Malaya where Malays and Chinese lived side by side throughout the entire land.

The riots were hardly over when Tan learned Lee was blaming Albar for them. Tan readily rushed to the UMNO Secretary General's defence. He had the MCA issue a statement saying Albar had never been anti-Chinese. The statement read: "In fact he is a champion of communal harmony."

In October 1964, after the trouble had subsided, Tan visited Singapore to try once again winning the friendship of the people there. In a public speech he told them that their 'vibrant state' had a bright future in Malaysia. "But Singapore cannot afford to be the sole oasis of prosperity in a desert of poverty. If Singapore prospers while the rest of Malaysia is retarded, Singapore will suffer in the long run," he remarked. He spoke of the problems of adjustment between Singapore and the Central Government, the misunderstandings, and of the need for ministers like him and the people of Singapore to get to know each other better. And then he referred to a 'wild rumour' which he said he had heard in Singapore – that Singapore could secede from Malaysia if it wished to do so. "This belief," said Tan, "is completely erroneous. There is no provision in the Constitution for any state to secede from the Federation."

Remembering that his own strength in Malaya came from the business community, Tan called on Singapore's businessmen to take a more active part in politics. Too many of them were concerned only with making money. He said there was a popular fallacy in Singapore that the people would only support a socialist philosophy. Because of this the men 'tainted by wealth' were unwilling to enter the political arena. Tan warned them that if there were too many men of talent making money and too few running the government, their money-making activities would not last very long.

Singapore's leaders reacted strongly to Tan's speech and denied that they were thinking of secession. They found it hard to believe that such rumours were circulating in Singapore and advised Tan that even if he had heard them, he would have been wiser not to help in spreading them.

The Straits Times gently suggested to Tan that the rumour was not worth all the attention he had given it. It commented: "There is a certain risk in taking rumours seriously, for an unsophisticated public is apt to think that there can be no smoke without fire, and however fantastic the rumour, it may begin to seem more credible when it gains the importance of public discussion."

When Tan rose to present his Budget in parliament on November 25, 1964, he tried hard to paint a cheerful picture of a booming economy expanding at the rate of five per cent a year. Indonesian Confrontation had shaken neither Malaysia's confidence in herself nor the world's confidence in Malaysia. The currency was stable.

But nothing could hide the big deficit in the Budget, or the inexorable rise in the cost of defence, or the steadily falling price of rubber – the main source of the country's revenue. The plain fact was that expenditure was increasing twice as fast as income. More money had to be found for health and education and rural development, especially in the new states of Sabah and Sarawak that had joined Malaysia believing it would carry them on wings into paradise.

Where was all this money to come from? Obviously from new taxes, however painful these might be. Tan tried to soften the blow by promising to cut down expenditure as far as possible. He drew attention to the steep rise in the cost of defence from $200 million in 1962 to $598 million. "This," he said," is a measure of our will to survive, whatever the cost."

He appealed to the country to follow the examples of Japan and Germany. Both had risen from defeat and destruction to perform economic miracles. "They pulled themselves up by their own efforts, and those efforts can be summed up in two qualities," he told a hushed chamber. "The first is hard work and the second is thrift. There is no doubt of tomorrow's sunshine. Equally, there is no doubt that it has to be earned by today's sweat and sacrifice."

There was nothing in the Finance Minister's speech that could quicken the heartbeat or warm the blood, no dazzling brilliance that could make people listen in wonder and cheer at the end. He was not that kind of speaker. He was not the artist who could make people tingle with a stroke of the brush. He was more like a bricklayer, placing his facts and figures one upon another till they formed a solid structure. Unexciting, perhaps, but neat and solid, a labour of love. Tan had spent days trying to impart to his speech the qualities he believed in – commonsense and sincerity. He was confident he had succeeded.

The reaction that came from Lee and his friends shocked Tan deeply. He found it vulgar. They scoffed at him, ridiculed his ideas and poured scorn on his new tax proposals. They appeared to him like political vandals who would not shirk at destroying their opponents. The PAP men recalled Tan's visit to Singapore in October and accused him of shaping his Budget to entice Singapore's businessmen. As he was a man of wealth, his financial policy must naturally reflect his own personal interests and those of his rich friends. Since he was wielding the axe, it had to fall on the less fortunate sections of the community. "But why do it so blatantly?" they asked.

The case of 'the dash and the comma' was, to Tan, a good example of the way his PAP rivals distorted his statements in their concerted move to ridicule him. In a speech in Parliament, Tan had referred to criticisms from the communists and their fellow travellers, as well as attacks from the Singapore Government, the PAP and trade unions under PAP control.

Lee's colleagues had, Tan averred, twisted this part of his speech and made it appear that he had accused the Singapore Government and the PAP of being fellow travellers.

"If they had taken the trouble to study that particular speech carefully," said Tan in his rejoinder, "they would have observed a comma and not a dash between the words 'fellow traveller' and the words 'the Singapore Government and the PAP'."

In spite of this explanation, a letter from Singapore appeared in one of the local newspapers, under the heading: 'The Sound of a Comma'.

The writer inquired: "May I ask what sounds Mr Tan made to indicate that he was using a comma instead of a dash when he delivered his speech?"

Tan quickly came to believe the PAP was involved in something far more dangerous than just a personal attack on him. Although Malaysia was at war and in desperate need of national unity, he was convinced Lee and his colleagues were launching a massive campaign to embarrass and undermine the central government for their own political advantage.

Tan accused Lee and his men of mobilizing the entire resources of the Singapore Government to inflame the people. The PAP men, he claimed, were twisting facts and distorting motives in public rallies and over Singapore's radio and television services.

From Tan's perspective they were trying to incite the people to action, perhaps even violent action, in order to bring the central government to its knees.

"These moves" said Tan, "are strange coming from men who say they are for Malaysia. They are doing everything they can to wreck proposals which are designed to ensure the survival of Malaysia."

As the bickering grew more intense the emphasis shifted from the new tax proposals to ugly racial issues. A vicious mood began to take hold of parliament. Tan noted that until the PAP had come along, parliament had always been a cheerful place, always able to dissolve tense moments with laughter. Lee and his friends, he decided, had changed that. Parliament was now filled with sullen resentment and hostility. Threats were now frequently made and nasty exchanges were becoming the norm.

Tan regarded reaction to the Budget as the first big test of the PAP's sincerity towards the wellbeing of Malaysia. "They have failed lamentably," he judged.

Syed Jaafar Albar.
UMNO Secretary General

Senu bin Rahman. As Director of
Election Affairs he was credited
with securing UMNO's stunning
polls victory in April, 1964.

Mohammed Khir Johari,
Malaysian Minister of Agriculture.

From the Singapore viewpoint the above were the Tunku's main 'hatchet men'.

THE FIGHT GOES ON

The Tunku had a priceless chuckle. It was a warm and friendly sound that brightened occasions and entertained audiences he wanted to reach. It often sent people helpless with laughter. He used this chuckle to amuse his friends and soften up his opponents. It was one of the reasons for his tremendous popularity. When Malaysians discussed the Tunku, they invariably ended up talking about his chuckle.

Many still remembered a notable occasion when this famous gift came to his rescue at a Rotary Club dinner in Kuala Lumpur. It was a big affair, attended by important men with bags of influence. The Rotarians had prevailed upon the Alliance leader to make a major policy speech. An adviser suggested the Tunku should try the American technique of putting his thoughts down on small cards no bigger than his palm. He could glance down casually at his hand now and then, and no one would know he was reading his speech. Just flip the cards aside, the Tunku was instructed, as he went along. The Tunku agreed.

It worked beautifully for twelve post-card pages. Then there was a pause, a long one. The twinkle in his eyes revealed something funny was happening. The chuckle came, started up from deep within. "Heh, heh, heh . . . where is page thirteen? I can't find page thirteen . . . heh, heh, heh . . . it doesn't matter. I don't think it's all that important . . . heh, heh, heh . . . I'll just carry on from page fourteen."

And so he did, while the serious-faced Rotarians dissolved in laughter.

The first signs of that chuckle always appeared in the Tunku's eyes. They suddenly lit up and brightened his face. But these eyes could also flash in anger. They could send a silent rebuke that could be more painful than harsh words.

On June 11, 1965, the Tunku's chuckle had deserted him. There was no laughter for his friends in the Press. His eyes were filled with dark clouds and his face lined with anxiety when he appeared at a press conference in his home. In a few hours he was to leave for London for the Commonwealth Prime Ministers' Conference. He was going with a very heavy heart.

"Why do we have to have all these quarrels?" he asked the reporters. "We are a happy country, a happy people. You can travel anywhere you like, and I don't think you will see the equal of Malaysia. Really, we have never had it so good."

Malaysia was starting to get the better of Indonesia's Confrontation. With national unity he could finish it off before very long. But if the internal quarrels continued, the Tunku intoned, they would give Sukarno and his communist friends fresh heart. Those responsible for the quarrels must remember that no matter how earnestly held their motives, they were helping the enemies of Malaysia.

The Tunku tapped the conference table as he began to talk about Lee Kuan Yew. "Mr Lee used to be sitting with me at this very table," the Malaysian prime minister recalled.

"We spent many late hours discussing many problems. All these problems that he raises now are not new. We discussed them fully before. In spite of everything he insisted on joining Malaysia. Now why bring up all these issues again! It is very bad."

The Tunku was distressed over a recent speech in which Lee allegedly drew attention to the phasing out of tribal chiefs in Africa and the collapse of the maharajahs in India. The Tunku took it to mean the Singapore leader was suggesting the same fate could befall the royal families in Malaysia. "You see the implications here!" said the Tunku. "It is not a very wise statement. It only causes unnecessary bad feeling among the people. Why do we want to say these things? If there is something bothering Mr Lee, I am ready to look into it and see if we can find a solution. Once before I spent hours listening to Mr Lee's proposals and reasons for letting Singapore join Malaysia. I am willing to spend hours listening to him again if that will help."

On his way to London, the Tunku stopped over for a few hours in Singapore and found a large crowd waiting to greet him at the airport. Lee, was there too with other PAP leaders. By this time, the Tunku was in a more cheerful mood. At the airport shops he bought a few portable TV sets for friends in Britain. He also had a light-hearted chat with Lee. There was laughter all round. It was an immensely encouraging scene after the gloomy press conference in Kuala Lumpur.

During his four hours in Singapore, the Tunku did not repeat a word of his earlier statement in Kuala Lumpur. Neither did he mention his offer to spend hours listening to any grievances Lee might wish to raise. The Singapore prime minister learned of it from a radio broadcast after giving the Tunku a hearty send-off. He felt elated believing he had somehow driven home his point.

Two days after the Tunku's departure, Lee was in high spirits when he spoke to some of his supporters. A few of the Tunku's underlings were still needling him but they didn't matter. From now on he would deal directly with the Tunku. Lee said he would wait for the Tunku to come back so that they could talk things over. In the meantime, if anything urgent should crop up, he would be prepared to talk to Tun Razak.

Lee felt it would be useful at this stage to add a warning to the 'hatchet men' and the slogan-shouting racial extremists in UMNO. These men were fond of using 'rough talk and strong, abrasive words'. But they should remember that the tougher they talked, the more difficult it would make things for themselves. "To these people I make this plea," Lee stated. "Be like the Tunku. Talk nicely, politely and calmly and win the hearts of the people of Singapore."

But the fight went on. In Kuala Lumpur, Albar was repeating his threat that the Malays would soon lose their patience. A junior political secretary hinted that the central government might take over control of the radio and television networks in Singapore.

Tan Siew Sin was threatening to close down the Bank of China in Singapore. He believed that Peking was using it to finance subversion in Malaysia. Lee challenged Tan to produce his evidence and warned him that closing the bank would mean cutting off all trade with China. Tan retorted that in such matters he had no need to consult the Singapore government. To this Lee replied: "Surely something more is required from the Finance Minister than to show that he is a boss man."

In Singapore, Lee and his colleagues were still talking about a Malaysian Malaysia, saying they had a cast-iron case and that the only way to save Malaysia was through a Malaysian solution. They continued to attack the *Utusan Melayu*, accusing it of pouring racial poison into the Malay villages. Singapore's Minister of Culture went after Albar, telling him it was a waste of time to talk about people losing their patience. They should pay more attention to not losing the argument.

Meanwhile, in London, the Tunku worried about the attitude of his Afro-Asian colleagues in the Commonwealth. He wanted them to say to Sukarno: "Stop your aggression, *now!*"

But many of them were not willing to do this. Some had written to him saying they were friends of both Malaysia and Indonesia and did not wish to get involved. They would prefer to see Malaysia and Indonesia get together and solve mutual problems on their own.

"But these countries," the Tunku fretted, "are blatantly disregarding the fact that Malaysia is the victim of this aggression. They must understand that no country should be allowed to commit aggression. If they value human rights and liberty they must do all they can to stop aggression."

The Tunku was also concerned about the Afro-Asian Conference which was to be held within a few weeks in Algiers. He wanted Malaysia to attend it but he was sure the Indonesians were bound to raise all kinds of obstacles. Without the help of its friends, Malaysia would not get a seat.

On June 18, the Tunku summoned all the passion he could muster when he delivered a speech in one of the sessions of the Commonwealth Prime Ministers' Conference. He referred to the Algiers gathering and appealed to his Afro-Asian colleagues for help to secure Malaysia's entry to it. Midway through his address, the president of Ghana applauded and called out: "Don't worry. You'll be there. You will be in."

This development called for a celebration. That night, the Tunku gave a dinner for a few friends at his Kensington flat. He cooked the main dishes himself – Malay style – with the help of his niece and the wife of the Sultan of Selangor.

The news from home was less heartening. UMNO men and PAP strongmen were still bickering and quarrelling as noisily as ever. In an interview with a Malaysian reporter, the Tunku blamed Lee for it all. There was bitterness in his voice when he confided: "At one period I felt that Confrontation would not continue because it was not doing the Indonesians any good, and many of them were aware of this. In discussions with prisoners, I found they had no heart to fight at all. Their leaders realised this and opposition to Confrontation was growing within Indonesia.

"In the midst of this, the PAP began a campaign of bringing up internal issues. This enabled the Indonesian leaders to say to their people, 'Take heart. We will crush Malaysia. It will break up by itself'. And so they continued Confrontation, although at one stage they were ready to give up."

In Singapore, Lee suddenly found himself with a by-election on his hands when an opposition member resigned from the State Legislative Assembly. Lee welcomed this opportunity to test his Party's stand, and decided that the PAP's election slogan would be – A Malaysian Malaysia.

On June 20, two days after the Tunku's dinner party in Kensington, Lee made a pungent speech to a gathering of tailors in Singapore. He told them that UMNO would prefer to see the non-Malays represented by boneless men. He exhorted them: "So I say to you: Let us stand firm now. A Malaysian Malaysia."

UMNO stalwarts were furious the following day when they received – accurately or not – the gist of Lee's speech and what he had purportedly remarked about the Malays. Lee was quoted as saying: "We believe every man can come up. Give him a chance. Open the doors, open the windows, and let fresh air blow through. He will learn and he will come up."

The quotation conveyed to UMNO continued: "But the attitude of the Malay traditionalists is different. They like to close the doors." The remainder of the report suggested the PAP leader had made further provocative remarks during his address.

Just as news of the UMNO interpretation of Lee's latest speech reached London, the Tunku, who had already been feeling a bit off-colour for days, felt worse. The 'ghostly snake' had begun its assault. The shingles made it difficult for him to walk and he was advised to stay in bed. It meant staying away from the Commonwealth Prime Ministers' Conference. It also gave him more time to study the situation back home.

When the Tunku entered the London Clinic on June 25, the Malaysian prime minister was understandably in a sombre mood. Apart from the shingles, his eyes were causing him much concern. He had glaucoma and he dreaded the likely suggestion of an eye operation.

The hospitalisation sparked a rumour that the Tunku would soon retire or go on extended leave. The prince from Kedah laughed when asked about it. "It will take more than an attack of shingles to make me retire," he replied. " I have many more years ahead of me and a long way to go. If I have to retire, it won't be now when the nation is in trouble."

In spite of the issues that kept him irksomely preoccupied, the Tunku responded immediately to the dying wish of an English woman who had once worked in the Malayan civil service. She had retired to Gloucester upon her retirement. When she heard Tunku Abdul Rahman was in London, she had gone, despite being terribly sick, to his hotel only to miss him. Too ill to wait, she returned home where she died the following day. Her dying wish, relayed by her husband, was for her ashes to be scattered over the jungles of Pahang which she had loved. When the Tunku was told of this, he promised to take her ashes back to Malaysia where a Royal Malaysian Air Force plane would scatter them over Pahang. This was carried out.

'Get well' wishes began to pour into the London Clinic for the Tunku. There was the one from Queen Elizabeth; another from Harold Wilson. There was also a message from Lee Kuan Yew. Many of these expressions of concern were delivered with large bouquets of flowers. Masses of roses, tulips, marigolds and carnations sprouted in the Tunku's hospital room. A correspondent wrote that the room glowed with all the colours of a belated summer. The Tunku himself remarked: "It's like the Chelsea flower show."

On June 27, the Tunku was still suffering from the pains of shingles and needed sedatives. Yet, in between naps, he appeared to be in high spirits and made a point of sounding extremely cheerful. Dressed in a purple and gold kimono, he sat up in bed and asked his photograph be taken by his private secretary in order to reassure people back home their leader was well and in command. He told his visitors: "I could play football right now."

But as was proved later it was all just an act. Behind the chirpy and animated demeanor lay thoughts that were fast dovetailing into a bitter decision.

More rioting in Singapore sees Malaysia's Deputy Prime Minister Tun Abdul Razak back on the island in September, 1964. He is shown here with Singapore's Deputy Prime Minister Dr Toh Chin Chye to his left. To Tun Razak's right, in a light safari suit, is Malaysia's Agriculture Minister Khir Johari.

A TO Z AND Z TO A

Tun Razak was the efficient, cautious plodder who made the Malaysian government machinery tick. He began his career in the colonial civil service where he acquired an admirable capacity for handling endless administrative work and a huge appetite for detailed, fiddly jobs. But in the current political life of Malaysia, he was very much the Tunku's deputy. It was widely accepted that, one day, he would become prime minister and perhaps he would come into his own. In the meantime, while waiting for his ultimate ascendancy, Tun Razak lived very much in the Tunku's shadow. He was a shorter, smaller man with a seemingly constant frown. He gave the impression of someone who found smiling a monumental task.

If Lee Kuan Yew was unprepared to accommodate the Tunku, he was even less willing to make concessions to a Tun Razak.

On June 29, Lee flew to Kuala Lumpur for talks with Razak to discuss a number of fundamental issues. The prospects were not bright. A few days earlier, an UMNO branch had advised the Tunku in London not to hold any talks with Lee. This was the view: "If you do, Lee will put on airs and behave as if he were your equal."

The central committee of the powerful UMNO Youth Movement, led by Senu bin Abdul Rahman, had held an emergency meeting and demanded a public apology from Lee for all he had said and done against the Malays. It insisted that until Lee apologized, neither the Tunku nor Razak should hold talks with him.

On the eve of the talks between Lee and Razak, Malaysia's *The Straits Times*, appealed to both men to defuse the bomb in their midst. It read: "That the controversy is dangerous is clear. Both sides admit it. There are moments when it begins to seem that only Indonesian Confrontation holds Malaysia together." The paper went on: "There has even been protest at the idea of talks at all. Not only must there be talks, there must be reaffirmation of the faith and trust which created Malaysia, and an end to the bitter exchanges which invite disaster. The mass media, which the governments control, must be muzzled. There are too many publicity agencies, political secretaries and headline seekers adding to the mischief. We are denying them the use of our columns."

Lee and Razak talked for nearly two hours, and came out smiling to meet the Press. According to Lee, they reviewed Malaysia's problems in a sober and earnest way, with no desire to score points off each other. "We had good discussions, frank and straightforward, on a number of basic issues," Lee told reporters. "Tun Razak suggesed we should talk again as we have many matters to discuss. We will then talk with the Tunku when he comes back."

Razak appeared to be in a hurry to officiate at an art exhibition. To reporters who asked him if he was happy with the talks, he replied: "You can say that."

Albar stood aloof from these proceedings. He was deeply resentful. In a signed statement, he said he was committed to the decision taken by the UMNO Youth Movement. "I have no confidence that any talks with Mr Lee will bring any good," he said. "To me, Mr Lee is one who cannot be trusted in view of his past and the tactics he has adopted."

In London the Tunku was still in pain. Dr Ismail who was with the Tunku's party, visited the prime minister and found that the shingles had taken much out of their leader. "Although the illness itself is not serious, it has strained the Tunku's health," the minister of internal security who also happened to be a medical doctor said afterwards. "He will need a fairly long period of convalescence."

Lying in his sick bed, the Tunku searched for an answer to the problems of Malaysia. "I had plenty of time to think – from A to

Z and backwards from Z to A – of our problems with Singapore," he recalled to confidants later. "I came to the conclusion that there would be no end to the bickering with Singapore except, perhaps, if Mr Lee Kuan Yew were made prime minister in the real sense of the word."

But how could there be two prime ministers in one country!

The repercussions of the squabble could be felt even in London. A number of Malaysian students studying in Britain were airing their discontent. Their young minds, to the Tunku's way of thinking, appeared to have been brainwashed. Also, wherever he turned, the Alliance leader perceived British and European press correspondents who were prejudiced and even hostile to his government.

He blamed Lee Kuan Yew for all this. Lee had misguided the students and misled the British Press. The Tunku was convinced that Lee would stop at nothing in his craving for power and as his frustration and bitterness increased, Lee would grow more dangerous. If he wanted so badly to be a prime minister in his own right, he could become one if Singapore became an independent state.

The Tunku drew up a balance sheet on Singapore. "I weighed the pros and cons of having Singapore in Malaysia," he said, adding, "I weighed the pros and cons of a Malaysia without Singapore".

On June 29, as Lee and Razak in Kuala Lumpur sought a road to reconciliation, the Tunku had made up his mind in London. He decided, with infinite sadness, that Singapore must leave Malaysia. He would say later: "For the wellbeing and security of Malaysia and Singapore, it is best that the two territories part. Otherwise there will be no hope of peace."

The Tunku would remember having opened his heart to Singapore's Minister of National Development, Lim Kim San, who was also travelling with him. Lim had dropped in to see him at the London Clinic "I took him into my confidence," said the Tunku, "I told him exactly how I felt about Singapore. No one can say that the Singapore government was not kept in the know."

On July 1, the Tunku sat up in bed and wrote a long letter to Tun Razak, setting out his feelings on Singapore. He asked his deputy to discuss the matter with a few senior members of the

Cabinet. His eyes filled with tears as he handed the letter to his personal secretary to post.

A week after his letter to Razak, the Tunku told a reporter in London that on his return to Malaysia, he would meet Lee Kuan Yew to smooth things over once and for all.

"We cannot afford to have differences within Malaysia at this time when we are being threatened by a common enemy," he said. He told the reporter he had asked Razak to find out what was troubling the Singapore leader, and to see if anything could be done to satisfy him without violating the constitution. "I will take over the talks when I return," he went on. "I will do everything in my power to bring about a quick settlement of this unnecessary trouble."

The Tunku was asked if the talks would lead to a political truce with Lee's PAP. He replied: "What is the use of a political truce? That is no way of settling our troubles. How can we negotiate a truce with a party that is not representative of all the races in Malaysia?'

In Singapore, the PAP's Rajaratnam welcomed the offer of talks with the Tunku, but added: "We wonder what the UMNO Youth will have to say on this."

Lee was busy leading his party in the Hong Lim by-election campaign which was now in full swing. He told supporters that a victory for the PAP would prove to the Tunku that the people of Singapore were all for a Malaysian Malaysia.

THE JOSEY AFFAIR

Alex Josey was a man who would be referred to in press releases as a British free lance journalist. But journalism was not Josey's main vocation. When he turned to it, much later in his professional life, it was to re-invent himself. Psychological warfare was his main occupation and that was the work he did when he was attached to the Royal Air Force in Cairo during World War II.

At the end of the war, he became Controller of News at Radio Jerusalem in Palestine, a job he left for a desk at the United Nations in Paris. The surfeit of diplomacy at the UN probably got to him immediately because it didn't take much for Sir Henry Gurney to lure him to work in Malaya. Gurney had been appointed high commissioner to the Emergency-ravaged peninsula. Sir Henry had been chief secretary of the Palestine government.

Josey was named psy-war adviser to General Sir Harold Briggs, Director of Operations, Malaya, the man who set out to starve the communists and their supporters by erecting brightly-lit, heavily guarded 'New Villages' behind coiled barbed wire.

Briggs resigned his office in 1951 and Gurney himself was assassinated in October, 1951. In the transition that saw General Sir Gerald Templer assume the twin roles of High Commissioner and Director of Operations, Josey's importance as psy-war expert was overlooked. This was probably the time when he took seriously to writing for a living.

He stayed on in Malaya and somehow managed to be re-employed by the government as an information specialist. In this capacity, he ran regular broadcasts over Radio Malaya where he explained why communism was inferior to parliamentary democracy. The talks were crisp and to the point, interesting and effective. They won him a big following.

His success as broadcast journalist did not last long. When it became known that Alex Josey was a keen socialist, the British businessmen in Malaya turned on him and lobbied that he be sacked; the sooner, the better. They seized on one of his daily broadcasts. It was an innocuous one but his paranoid critics chose to interpret it as a subtle proposal to nationalise the Malayan rubber plantations which were largely owned by British companies. The rubber barons felt betrayed by one of their kind. A fearful row broke out and Radio Malaya did not offer Josey another contract.

He based himself in Singapore and got hired as a stringer for a few British newspapers. He began to grow a bushy beard, confirming to minds used to stereotypes about the ferocity of his socialist leanings. Better that he was out of Malaya!

Alex Josey was a survivor. He survived Palestine and he was determined to survive Malaya. Soon he had attached himself to the PAP leaders. In Singapore, what he sold was his adroitness at handling the international press. He became a useful man to have around especially on overseas trips, a boon to an emerging city state eager to establish its credentials to the world. He was very useful in the lead-up to merger.

But he seemed unable to get it right with Kuala Lumpur. In October, 1963, Josey found himself at the centre of another storm. *The Bulletin* news magazine in Australia ran an article under his by-line where he compared Lee Kuan Yew with Tunku Abdul Rahman. Lee, Josey wrote, belonged to a race with thousands of years of culture, while the Tunku's ancestors were people with no great tradition other than piracy.

There were angry protests from UMNO but the Tunku took it light-heartedly.

The Malayan leader responded: "I passed this off good-humouredly saying that I was proud of my ancestors in as much as the British made heroes of their pirates like Sir Francis Drake and others."

But the incident was never forgotten.

On July 7, 1965, the Malaysian Cabinet decided to expel Alex Josey for interfering in the internal affairs of Malaysia. He

Alex Josey in his journalistic role. This picture was taken on June 30, 1965, outside Singapore's Victoria Memorial Hall on nomination day for prospective candidates in the island's Hong Lim by-election.

Alex Josey and powerful friends. Here Josey is shown enjoying a game of golf with Singapore's then Defence Minister Goh Keng Swee and the island's then Finance Minister Lim Kim San.

was given 14 days to leave the country. His lawyers advised him there could be no appeal against the expulsion order.

"What does this mean?" Lee demanded, when he heard the news. "Is this just to make foreign correspondents more amenable to reporting favourably on the Central Government? Or is this, at the same time, a hint to those who are friendly with these correspondents?"

In Singapore, the Foreign Correspondents' Association of Southeast Asia, of which Josey was a member, expressed its 'deepest concern' and asked for a full public explanation. It said the expulsion was a grave threat to journalism as a profession and infringed the democractic principles which Malaysia claimed to respect.

In London, *The Times* described the action as a sign of weakness and ill-temper: "Mr Josey has been told to go within 14 days because his going will be conducive to the good of the Federation. Such mumbling reasons carry no weight at all."

When first approached, the Tunku refused comment. His spokesman explained the leader was unable to say anything as the decision had been made in his absence. But, 24 hours later, the Tunku issued a long statement in which he accused Josey of trying to disrupt Malaysia's inter-racial harmony. He even recalled *The Bulletin* article where Josey had claimed the Malays were descendants of pirates.

"There have been incorrect reports by various foreign correspondents from time to time in the past but we were prepared to overlook these mistakes because we saw no ulterior motives behind their writing, other than sheer carelessness or lack of information," the Tunku's statement read.

It continued: "In the case of Mr Josey, however, he is not a free-lance in the proper sense of the word. He has persisted in his attempts to stir up trouble among the races in a very subtle manner in keeping with his background as an expert in psychological warfare."

About the same time as the Tunku was issuing this statement in London, Singapore's Deputy Prime Minister Toh Chin Chye summoned an emergency press conference. With him were several other ministers of the Singapore government.

Toh described the expulsion of Josey as only the first step towards the suppression of liberalism in Malaysian politics. "If the Central Government continues to placate its extremists, further repressive measures must be taken which must lead to the break-up of Malaysia," he declared.

He said the extremists were also demanding the arrest and detention of Lee Kuan Yew. "We know that soon after the last meeting of Parliament and the first public rally of the Malaysia Solidarity Convention, instructions were given to make a case for Mr Lee's arrest," said Toh. The PAP, he continued, urged the central government not to believe that with Mr Lee out of the way, the ministers of the PAP government will quietly acquiesce in his detention. "The Alliance leaders must realise that Malaysia will break up if any such repressive action is taken," he added.

Approached by reporters for comment a few hours later, Razak refused to touch on Toh's charges. He issued a statement the following day. "The allegations by the PAP are too wild and mischievous to merit any comment," he stated. He reminded the Press that at the previous meeting of Parliament he had warned Lee not to stir up racial unrest. Otherwise, he would be held responsible for any trouble that broke out.

In a sharp retort, Lee asked Razak not to beat about the bush. "Did they, or did they not, order a case for my arrest? Why don't they answer that?"

The answer came from London, from the Tunku, who was now fit enough to swing his legs about 'like a footballer'.

"As far as I know," the Malaysian prime minister said, "there is no evidence against Mr Lee to warrant his arrest or detention." But he advised Lee and his colleagues not to make wild guesses that could further sour relations between Singapore and the central government.

"Malaysia has enjoyed peace and harmony," added the Tunku. "Let us keep it that way. If we have to quarrel among ourselves, let it be on an issue that is worth quarrelling about. But let it not be on Alex Josey who is not even a citizen of our country."

The Tunku also defended UMNO 'Ultras' who had been accused by Lee of causing all the trouble. He remarked: "There are 'Ultras' in every party and the PAP itself is not free of them. Without 'Ultras' the party will not have life. It will be devoid of all political spirit. To me, the UMNO Youth have been a great help to the party. Their loyalty is something of which I am proud."

In the meantime, the Josey affair continued to make angry headlines, especially in Britain. Paul Johnson, editor of *The New Statesman*, called on the Tunku and tried to persuade him to withdraw the expulsion order. Johnson said later: "It didn't take much cross-questioning to see that the reasons he publicly gave for expelling Josey were not the real ones, and that in fact Josey is being made a sacrificial victim to appease the fanatical anti-Chinese elements in the Tunku's party. If the Tunku doesn't feel strong enough to resist them on this issue, where will he draw the line?"

Johnson felt that any attempt to arrest Lee would destroy multi-racialism in Malaysia and perhaps provoke civil war. This would raise the whole question of the British presence in Malaysia.

The New Statesman editor went on: "It is one thing to spend £400 million (sterling) a year defending Malaysian democracy against Indonesian aggression – quite another to underwrite, at such cost, a state which turns its back on basic constitutional rights and lurches towards racism. Things have not come to this pass, but the trend is ominous."

A report from Josey himself in the same publication claimed his expulsion resulted from a secret meeting of Malay extremists in the house of Senu bin Abdul Rahman, the 'bald-headed UMNO Youth leader'. Albar was also present. According to Josey, they decided to ask for his immediate expulsion and called on Razak not to hold talks with Lee. This put Razak in a spot. He was already under instructions from the Tunku to see Lee. The report said that Razak had to decide whether to obey the Tunku, the moderate, or Albar, the extremist. Razak compromised and saw Lee, but agreed to order Josey out.

Josey believed that the Malay extremists were openly challenging the Tunku's leadership and his policy of tolerance and moderation. Josey's reading was that if the Tunku were ousted, Lee's position in Singapore would become uncertain. And if Lee went, the CPM would move in and would probably be welcomed as defenders by the majority of the non-Malays.

Josey's conclusion: "If, on the other hand, the Tunku stands firm, cleanses UMNO of extremists and reshuffles his cabinet,

Singapore's leading political figures and locally-based foreign correspondents are on hand to farewell Alex Josey at a dinner party held in the island's Sri Temasek. Kuala Lumpur has given Josey two weeks to leave Singapore. This picture, taken on July 18, 1965, shows the bearded Josey sitting to the right of Prime Minister Lee Kuan Yew.

Senior Singapore politician, S. Rajaratnam, escorted his personal friend Alex Josey to a passenger airliner bound for Britain on July 20, 1965. Josey was departing Paya Lebar airport on expulsion orders from Kuala Lumpur. His absence, however, was short-lived. After the island state's own expulsion from the Federation a matter of days thereafter, Josey returned to live and work in independent Singapore until 1984. He died in 1986 of complications from Parkinson's Disease.

he and Mr Lee together could make Malaysia work and Britain's immense current expenditure on the defence of Malaysia would be worthwhile."

The day after the publication of Josey's piece, Senu lashed out at both Josey and Johnson. Josey, he said, had dreamed up the story that Malay extremists were challenging the Tunku's leadership, that he was obviously trying to split the Malays between so-called moderates and extremists. This, he claimed, was further evidence of Josey's meddling in Malaysia's internal affairs.

Senu explained that there was nothing secret about the meeting in his house. In fact, a press statement was issued the following day. The decision to expel Josey was taken not at that meeting but by the Cabinet after careful study. The Tunku was kept informed and approved the decision.

Turning to Johnson, Senu asked: "Does he believe that the whole issue of the British presence in Malaysia depends solely on one man – Mr Lee Kuan Yew? If the answer is yes, then the people of Malaysia will know the relationship between the British and Mr Lee, and what game the British have been playing in this country. Mr Johnson's comments are an insult to Malaysia and Malaysians."

Kuala Lumpur backed Senu with a public statement: "The latest biased articles by an English editor and Josey himself are mischievous and calculated to embarrass and undermine the leaders of Malaysia in the eyes of people overseas. Josey's article only confirms that all along he has been indulging in the internal politics of our country." It added that the Tunku was in complete agreement with the Cabinet decision to expel Josey. "The Josey case," it ended, " is closed as far as the central government is concerned."

DESTINATION DISASTER

On July 10, the people of Hong Lim in Singapore went to the polls to elect a new representative for their constituency. The former member had resigned, causing a by-election. There were two candidates for his seat – one from Lee's PAP and the other from the pro-communist *Barisan Socialis* party which was still echoing Sukarno's threat to crush Malaysia.

Hong Lim was an unpredictable sort of place, but on July 10, it seemed to offer one thing with certainty: a close fight which could go either way. The gambling men, usually active on such occasions, were nervous. Only a handful of them were willing to offer or accept bets, and they were all putting their money on the *Barisan Socialis.*

The PAP won by a comfortable margin. Lee, flushed with victory, invited the men in UMNO to ponder over the results. Sixty per cent of the voters of Hong Lim had backed the PAP and given it a mandate 'beyond any doubt' to fight for a Malaysian Malaysia. But 40 per cent had voted for the *Barisan Socialis* which wanted to destroy Malaysia.

To Lee Kuan Yew and the rest of the PAP, the message was clear. If there was not going to be a Malaysian Malaysia, and if the 60 per cent lost faith in it, the results of the next election would be very different!

Senu was not impressed. He warned Lee that just because the Malays were polite and courteous, they should not be considered weak and easily pushed around.

"We Malays are not without intelligence and ability," he stressed. "What we want is opportunity, the opportunity to obtain

The PAP's ultimately successful Hong Lim by-election candidate, Lee Koon Choy, is lifted shouder-high by supporters outside Singapore's Victoria Memorial Hall following the submission of his papers on nomination day, June 30, 1965.

economic wealth for our people." Senu strongly resented Lee's habit of saying that he was in Malaysia not by anyone's favour but in his own right. "The right which Lee is enjoying today," argued Senu, "did not fall from the sky or out of the blue. It was given to him. Doesn't he have some feeling of gratitude to the natives of this country?"

"No," Lee replied as emphatically. "I am not enjoying anyone's hospitality. I am here as of right. And 61 per cent of the people of Malaysia have to stand by that or it is lost. Without it they would have no future."

Lee felt that it was now up to the Tunku to settle the argument so that Malaysia could get on with the job of economic development. The first task would be to stop the racial slurs being put out every day by the *Utusan Melayu*.

By this time, the Tunku, free of shingles, had moved from London to a health resort near the French Alps for a fortnight's rest. Here he waited for a reply from Razak to his July 1 letter. The reply arrived on July 22. Razak said he had consulted his senior Cabinet colleagues and they were in full agreement with the Tunku that Singapore should leave Malaysia and go its own way.

The Tunku slept on this for three days. On July 25, he wrote to Razak again, this time asking him to go ahead with the legal and constitutional preparations for the removal of Singapore from the federation.

Razak cabled back that he would convene Parliament on August 9 to make the necessary amendments to the Malaysian Constitution. The bill for this purpose would be tabled on a certificate of urgency, which meant that it would be presented, debated and approved at once. The Attorney General was instructed to start work on the bill immediately.

After reading this cable, the Tunku felt more relaxed in France. He would recall: "I visited the casinos just to while away the time. When I entered, people all around looked up and murmured, 'Here is an Eastern potentate. He's coming to throw away his money on the gaming tables'. On one occasion I was terribly ashamed when I placed a bet of five francs. The croupier looked at me in amazement, because he expected nothing so small, as the minimum bet was ten francs." The Tunku laughed. "However," he mused, "although I am poor in wealth, I am rich in friends."

Back home, a new row had blown up. Tan Siew Sin, was demanding 60 per cent of the Federal revenue collected in Singapore. This had been the issue which nearly wrecked the Malaysia talks in London in 1963. At that time Singapore had argued stubbornly for 39 per cent but had finally agreed to 40 per cent to save the conference from total collapse. This was the figure in the Malaysia Agreement. But Tan, representing the central government, was now going back to his old demand for 60 per cent. He claimed the money was needed to meet the increasing costs of defence and development.

Singapore's Finance Minister Goh Keng Swee rejected Tan's demand. Goh argued that the brunt of Indonesian Confrontation had fallen on Singapore which had lost 15 per cent of its trade. In fact, instead of paying more to the central government, Singapore was hoping to reduce the amount from 40 to 30 per cent.

The Singaporean also pointed out that Singapore's contribution was closely linked with political factors. Singapore with 1.9 million people had only 15 seats in the Malaysian Parliament, whereas Sabah and Sarawak with 1.2 million people had 40 seats.

Kuala Lumpur accused Singapore of not showing the right spirit when faced with a dangerous enemy. Goh, in turn, accused the central government of trying to strangle the island's infant industries and, at the same time, using pressure to prevent the introduction of new industries there. To prove his point, he quoted an extract from the annual report of an Australian company which said: "Factories were automatically encouraged to be on the mainland instead of Singapore. One is inclined to the view that this is intentional and brought about by inter-governmental jealousies."

Tan replied that it was Singapore which had shown utter disregard for the rest of Malaysia. All that the central government was trying to do was to ensure that the whole of Malaysia, and not Singapore alone, benefited from the industrialization programme.

The quarrel subsided but there remained a lot of bad feeling.

On July 25, Razak visited Singapore and toured an outlying area inhabited by Malay fishermen and peasants. Three days earlier, the Malaysian deputy prime minister had written to the Tunku in France, agreeing to the expulsion of Singapore from Malaysia.

The day he was touring the fishing villages, the Tunku was writing back, asking him to proceed with arrangements for the removal of Singapore as he had indicated in the July 22 letter.

Razak did not say a word about these moves to the large Malay crowds which turned up to greet him. Instead he spoke about the central government's efforts to help the Malays in the rest of Malaysia.

Under the Rural Development Programme, said Razak, Malays were being given homes and ten acres of high-yielding rubber or oil palm in new land schemes. A new agency was helping to lead the Malays into commerce and industry. The *Bank Bumiputra* – Bank for the Natives – had been sponsored by the government to give them loans for this purpose.

"There are now more roads, mosques, schools and so on in the villages than since we first got independence," Razak told his listeners. "Improvements have been tremendous and the benefits to the Malays have been very great."

Razak also said he wanted to extend these benefits to the Malays in Singapore, but had come up against an obstacle. The Singapore authorities under Lee were not prepared to cooperate and this was holding up everything.

The allegation provoked an outburst from Lee who said he knew of no plans by the central government to improve the areas which Razak had just visited. In fact, the only thing he had heard of was a proposal to buy an estate in another area and the Singapore government had assisted in this. If Razak could give any instance of delay, the PAP leader challenged, he would immediately put the matter right.

Lee said it was a great pity that Razak had chosen to make such a statement while touring a Malay area. He was clearly insinuating that the Singapore government was trying to prevent the central government from helping the Malays in Singapore. Not only was this unfounded, but it was also designed to increase communal suspicions.

"The truth is quite the contrary," said Lee. "The Singapore government welcomes competition by the central government to see who can do better, to see who has more practical development projects for the Malays and for other communities in Singapore."

Razak brushed aside the challenge and invited Lee to work hand in hand with the central government. "There should be no question of competing against each other," Tun Razak stated. "Once that happens, difficulties will arise. If both the state and central governments work together, we will be able to carry out development schemes for the people."

But Singapore was keen to compete, believing that everyone would benefit from healthy competition. Without it, the nation would not progress; in fact, it would slip into reverse and regress.

While all these exchanges were being made, Lee was pushing harder than ever for a Malaysian Malaysia.

"I am sure that ten years from now there will be fewer racial problems because by then the people will have become used to this concept of a Malaysian Malaysia," he announced optimistically. "But meanwhile," he encouraged his listeners, "we must say it openly and loudly – that all Malaysians are owners of Malaysia – in order to drive home this concept."

THE FINAL ACT

On August 5, 1965, the Tunku returned home after nearly eight weeks abroad. Although it was about four o'clock in the morning when his plane landed in Singapore, there were five hundred UMNO supporters at the airport to welcome him.

The crowd had waited for more than ten hours because the leader's plane had developed engine trouble and was delayed in Karachi.

Despite the early hour, the Tunku's followers appeared to be buoyed by the bannered greetings they waved to the returning prime minister. Apart from the ordinary welcoming tidings, UMNO supporters also carried placards denouncing Lee Kuan Yew.

Lee Kuan Yew is destroying peace and harmony.
Discuss nothing with the traitor.
We don't want Singapore to become a Palestine.
Lee Kuan Yew is a snake with two heads.
Crush Lee Kuan Yew.

The Tunku was quick to advise the assembly to do nothing that would disrupt the peace. In a democratic country there were bound to be hot words bandied around now and then, he told them in his usual fatherly fashion. This was all right so long as no one went beyond the bounds of justice.

The Tunku said that in spite of the placards, he would have to meet Lee to try to settle the differences between Singapore and the central government. First, though, he needed a rest. He was very tired.

Lee was away that morning, holidaying with his family in the Cameron Highlands in central Malaya. His minister of national development, Lim Kim San, went to the airport to greet the Tunku on behalf of the Singapore government.

Later in the day, after a rest in Singapore, the Tunku flew to Kuala Lumpur where a hero's welcome awaited him. He was garlanded and members of the UMNO Youth Movement showered rice on him, a token of happiness at seeing him back. Then all heads were bowed in a prayer of gratitude for *Bapa Malaysia's* safe return.

The Tunku looked extremely fit and cheerful. He was obviously delighted to be home with family and friends. There were kisses and hugs for his little grandchildren and a broad smile for everyone else. He moved around with a sprightly step, garlands dangling from his neck.

During a press conference at the Kuala Lumpur airport, the Tunku talked about Singapore again. He told reporters: "When I've had a short rest, I will send for Mr Lee and I will listen to his complaints. I don't know what his problems are. Though certain UMNO members have urged me not to see Mr Lee, I feel it is my responsibility to meet him and try to ensure peace in the country. This is because everyone is looking up to me as the father of the nation and hoping that I can settle the squabble."

To a reporter who doubted if a settlement was possible, the Tunku replied: "If it is possible now for a man to go to the moon, I don't see why we cannot find ways to resolve our troubles." He pointed out that there had been no riots or disturbances of any kind during his absence, which meant that the situation was not as serious as some had made it out to be. He had handled more difficult problems before, and he was confident he could deal with the present ones.

The Tunku's remarks created a feeling of wellbeing. Lee's PAP responded enthusiastically, saying it had always been ready for talks with the Tunku. The *Malay Mail*, like other publications, was optimistic. "With Tunku Abdul Rahman home again," the daily stated, "the heat of political exchange between Kuala Lumpur and Singapore should quickly subside."

But the Tunku's cheerful smiles and bright remarks were really hollow – as would be revealed later. In fact he had returned home from his overseas trip with a deep sense of foreboding. He could 'feel' Malaysia heading rapidly towards racial unrest and bloodshed.

In such a situation, Malaysia's leaders would normally fall back on the Special Branch for information and guidance. But this time the Special Branch had nothing significant to report. As far as it was concerned, the situation was quiet and under control.

Yet the Tunku's instinct was flashing a warning signal to him and he believed his instinct had never been wrong. As a betting man, he would rather put his money on his instinct than on the Special Branch. He had followed it throughout his career and it had served him well.

His instinct was now warning him of imminent danger. Still physically exhausted from his flight, he went straight to bed and slept till early evening when Tun Razak arrived with a big file.

The two leaders talked for two hours. During their discussions, Razak described his meeting with Lee and analyzed the situation. The picture he painted was extremely bleak.

The Tunku had more talks with Razak the following day, August 6. This time other senior members of the Cabinet joined them. Dr Ismail and Tan Siew Sin were both in attendance. So, too, was Minister of Works, Posts and Telecommunications V.T. Sambanthan, President of MIC, third partner of the Alliance. The 'Big Five' had gathered.

The decision was unanimous: the situation with Singapore was hopeless. Singapore must go.

This was conveyed that same evening to Goh Keng Swee, who had arrived in Kuala Lumpur with other PAP leaders. Lee, who was still relaxing in the cool, brisk air of the Cameron Highlands, was promptly informed that an ultimatum had been delivered – Singapore must leave Malaysia or the situation would get out of control. He hurried down to Kuala Lumpur for consultations with his colleagues.

At noon the following day, August 7, Lee and Goh drove to the Residency for a meeting with the Tunku and found him with Razak and the other members of the 'Big Five'. As Lee wanted to talk privately with the Tunku, they adjourned to an inner room for half an hour.

Once again, the Tunku explained to Lee that his campaign for a Malaysian Malaysia had caused racial feelings to rise almost to flashpoint. He said he would not be able to control events if Singapore insisted on staying in Malaysia.

Lee pleaded for another way out. He proposed a looser federation in which Singapore would feel more comfortable, but the Tunku replied that even this was no longer possible.

The Singapore leader then told the Tunku that some of his colleagues who had family ties in the peninsula felt very strongly about Malaysia and would refuse to leave unless they were convinced it was the only solution. He requested the Tunku write a brief note to Toh Chin Chye particularly explaining the position.

The Tunku agreed to do this, then walked away to feed his goldfish, ending the discussion.

In his letter to Toh, the Tunku wrote:

My Dear Chin Chye,

I am writing to tell you that I have given the matter of our break with Singapore my utmost consideration and I find that in the interest of our friendship and security and peace of Malaysia as a whole, there is absolutely no other way out.

If I were strong enough and able to exercise complete control of the situation, I might perhaps have delayed action, but I am not, and so, while I am able to counsel tolerance and patience, I think an amicable settlement of our difficulties in this way is the only possible way out.

I request you most earnestly to agree.

Kind regards,
Tunku Abdul Rahman

To this a disheartened, disillusioned Toh replied:

My Dear Tunku,

I thank you for your undated letter which I received yesterday explaining your position and your

188

solution to the present difficulties that have arisen between the Central Government and the Singapore government. It is indeed sad that in your view our problems can be solved only by asking Singapore to quit Malaysia and this barely two years from the day Malaysia was inaugurated.

My colleagues and I would prefer that Singapore remain in Malaysia and we felt that there could be other solutions to the present impasse.

However, as you have indicated that the situation does not lend itself to any other workable settlement and as you have impressed upon me that Singapore remaining in Malaysia will lead to a situation you may not be able to control, we have no alternative but to be resigned to your wish that Singapore leaves the Federation of Malaysia.

I and my colleagues had rejoiced at the reunification of Singapore with Malaya in September 1963. It has come as a blow to us that the peace and security of Malaysia can only be served by the expulsion of Singapore from Malaysia. If this is the price for peace in Malaya and Singapore then we must accept it, however agonizing our inner feelings may be.

Although lasting unification of Singapore and Malaya has not been achieved this time, nevertheless it is my profound belief that future generations will succeed where we have failed. In order that my friends and political colleagues in the other states of Malaysia and particularly in the Malaysian Solidarity Convention may know my true feelings on this matter, I may have at some future date to tell them of the true position.

With kind regards,
Toh Chin Chye.

After his meeting with the Tunku, Lee flew back to Singapore with the Separation Agreement which had already been drawn up. He promised the Tunku he would have it signed and returned the following day.

The frenzied activity was noted and rumours began to fly around but the guesses were way off the mark. One newspaper even reported that Lee was about to resign to make way for a more moderate leader who could improve relations with Kuala Lumpur.

On Sunday, August 8, the chief ministers of the various states were summoned to a secret meeting in Kuala Lumpur. They could hardly believe their ears when the Tunku broke the news to them. Anyone who might have wished to protest realised it would be futile to do so.

All other Alliance MPs were instructed to be present in Parliament the following morning, August 9, to vote for an important government motion. They were not told what it would be.

Albar demanded more information before he pledged his support. He was rebuffed.

Later that Sunday evening the Tunku and some of his closest colleagues held a private dinner party in a penthouse in one of the tallest buildings in Kuala Lumpur. It was a place where they could count on being left to themselves. A small band provided soothing, Malay music in the traditional style.

As the evening wore on the Tunku and his friends began to perform Malay dances. Their partners were a group of cultural dancing girls who were often engaged, even at official parties, to dance with the guests. The numbers called for no physical contact between dancing partners.

In the middle of all the merriment, an obviously distressed man in a bright Hawaiian shirt burst on the scene.

The gatecrasher was Lord Head, the British High Commissioner to Malaysia. Sometime during the day he had heard rumours about Singapore's expulsion from the federation. He had tried frantically to contact the Tunku, only to realise that the Malaysian politician would not be talked out of his decision and therefore made a point of avoiding him.

Lord Head had reasons to be unusually upset. Britain had been closely involved in the setting up of Malaysia. At tremendous cost to herself, she was bearing the brunt of Malaysia's defence against Indonesian Confrontation. Her main military strength was based in Singapore and the island was vital to the defence of Malaysia. How would the British public react when they discovered

Britain had not even been informed about this major upheaval? But, more importantly, the separation would provide Sukarno a stunning psychological victory.

When Lord Head finally learned of the Tunku's whereabouts, he dashed to the penthouse. Too much was at stake to bother about protocol.

The Tunku was peeved but agreed to see him. He took Lord Head aside and they were joined by Razak and the other members of his 'Big Five'.

They talked earnestly for a few minutes. Then the Tunku left the group and began dancing again. Nobody noticed it when the Malaysian prime minister slipped out quietly. Lord Head realised he had failed.

At ten o'clock on Monday, August 9, 1965, Lee Kuan Yew stood on the steps of Singapore's City Hall. Around him were members of the press and the diplomatic corps who had been summoned for an urgent briefing.

> *"Singapore shall forever be a sovereign, democratic and independent nation founded upon the principles of liberty and justice and forever seeking the welfare and happiness of its people in a more just and equal society."*

Everyone was stunned when Lee proclaimed that Singapore had ceased to be a state within Malaysia.

At precisely the same time, Radio Singapore announced the news to the people of the island. In some places it was greeted with the thunderous explosion of firecrackers – the traditional Chinese way of celebrating a joyous occasion. On the Singapore Stock Exchange, there was a sudden upsurge of activity and prices began to soar.

But Lee felt deep sorrow. His eyes brimmed with tears when, later in the day, he appeared at a televised press conference held in the local TV studios on Caldecott Hill. He talked bravely about Singapore's future but could not contain himself when he tried to explain the events leading to its break with Malaysia.

"Every time we look back to the moment we signed this document, it is for us a moment of anguish. For me it is a moment of anguish. All my life, my whole adult life, I have believed in merger and unity of the two territories ..."

His voice began to falter. "We are connected by geography, economics and ties of kinship. It broke everything we stood for ... " Tears rolled down his cheeks and he buried his face in his hands for a moment. He tried to continue but his voice broke again. He apologized; he was too upset to go on.

Later he talked about his final meeting with the Tunku. As he left, the Tunku had said to him: "Well, you know, when you are no longer in Malaysia and we are not quarrelling in Parliament or in the constituencies, we shall be friends again. We shall need each other and we shall cooperate."

Lee said he earnestly hoped it would be so.

At half-past-nine on Monday, August 9, 1965, the Tunku summoned all Alliance MPs to a committee room in Parliament House in Kuala Lumpur and broke the news to them. He told them that within half an hour he would introduce a bill in Parliament to amend the constitution so that Singapore could leave Malaysia. The bill would need a two-thirds majority and they would all have to vote for it.

Albar began to fume quietly. He had always believed in keeping Singapore in its proper place, by tough action if necessary. He believed that the Malay Regiment could easily cope with Singapore and whip it into line. Letting Singapore leave Malaysia was utter madness. Malaysia could not afford to have such a close neighbour controlled by an independent and hostile government.

At ten o'clock the Tunku strode into Parliament. The House was packed and tense. He began his speech at once.

He said: "What I am about to announce to this House will no doubt come as a big surprise and shock to members. In fact, to me and to many members, it is the most painful and heartbreaking news I have had to break."

He spoke about his efforts to reach an understanding with Lee and his colleagues. "It appeared that as soon as one issue was resolved, another cropped up. Where a patch was made here, a tear appeared elsewhere, and where one hole was plugged

More than a decade later – 1976 to be exact – and old differences of opinion are apparently forgotten. The now Tan Sri Syed Jaafar Albar (right) shakes hands with Dato Musa Hitam, the man who replaced him as UMNO Secretary General following his forced resignation in August, 1965.

another leak appeared. It seemed completely impossible to arrive at a solution."

In the end he had found only two courses of action open to him. He could either take repressive action against the Singapore government, or break off all ties with it since it had ceased to show even the slightest loyalty to the central government.

The Tunku said he decided against taking repressive measures because this was "repulsive to our concept of parliamentary democracy." In any case, he declared, it would not have worked.

He told a hushed Parliament: "The seed of contempt, fear and hatred has been sown in Singapore, and even if we try to prevent its growth, I feel that after a time it will sprout up in a more virulent form."

He accused the foreign press of running a campaign to belittle him and his government while building up Lee's image. Some foreign governments as well had encouraged Lee to regard himself as the Tunku's equal, making things very awkward for the Malaysian leader.

"There can only be one Prime Minister for the nation, and so the best course we could take was to allow Lee Kuan Yew to be the Prime Minister of an independent Singapore in the full sense of the word," he added.

The Tunku talked about his dream to make Singapore the 'New York of Malaysia'. He had begged the politicians in Singapore to work for this instead of their own personal glorification. Unfortunately, political rivalry had made this impossible.

"My dream is shattered and so we come now to the parting of the ways," he remarked.

Looking to the future, the Tunku promised he would do all he could to help Singapore. He said, "In diversity I am convinced we can find unity. Or in ordinary every day parlance, absence will make hearts grow fonder."

Tan Siew Tin, speaking after the Tunku in Parliament, painted a grim picture. Those in possession of the full facts know that unless something was done quickly, there would be widespread racial violence, he announced. Racial tension, he informed the House, had risen alarmingly and in 17 years of active politics he had never known the situation to be so dangerous.

"A Sino-Malay clash in Malaysia on a large scale, with the two races roughly equal in number and scattered all over the country, and in many places inextricably mixed, would have been the kind of holocaust beside which racial riots in other countries might appear to be a mere picnic," he concluded.

The final act produced an ironic twist.

When the vote on the Separation Bill was taken, Albar was missing. He had obviously stayed away in protest. The Tunku was furious and decided to sack him from his post as Secretary General of UMNO, but softened when some of his senior colleagues pleaded on Albar's behalf. He agreed to let Albar resign.

Later, at a press conference, the Tunku spoke sadly about his problems with Singapore. With a mournful smile he said: "We are human beings. I say if you marry a pretty girl and don't get on well with her, you've got to divorce her."

The Tunku also spoke about his intuition which had influenced his final decision.

"I can sense, feel and smell like a stable boy who knows his horse," he said. "He is part of the horse and usually knows whether it will win or not. In the same way, I feel that I am part of this country and I also feel that the course we have taken is right."

The Press was keen to know what Lee thought about Albar's situation. The Tunku replied that if Albar had been sacked at the time of the riots in Singapore the previous year, the separation would not have taken place.

But what good was that kind of talk now?

In London, the British government was shocked and apprehensive. The separation could mean more trouble in the area. *The Times* wrote: "The departure – and the emergence – of so politically conscious and economically active a unit (as Singapore) throws the whole future of Malaysia into doubt and with it British policies in Southeast Asia."

Washington was startled and began a full-scale review of the situation in Southeast Asia. *The Washington Post* said: 'The withdrawal of Singapore is a very sad thing indeed. It means a very severe weakening of Malaysia itself, for Singapore was its prosperous and energetic lynchpin."

Australia was clearly disappointed. *The Sydney Morning Herald* read: 'Those, who from the very beginning, have considered

Malaysia an artificial creation set up by foreign forces, received today more unmistakable evidence that they were right."

The only jubilant note came from Jakarta. Sukarno cheered the split and said he had been proved right all along. The merger between Singapore and Malaya was an aberration, a freak which could not survive.

December 12, 1989. A quiet exchange in less frenzied times. Prime Minister Lee Kuan Yew hears of the Tunku's illness and visits his former political foe. By this time the Tunku is in his 19th year of retirement from the Malaysian leadership. The following year, Lee himself will relinquish his prime ministerial post to become Singapore's Senior Minister. The Tunku died in December, 1990.

Photo Credits

p. 4, The New Straits Times; p. 6, The New Straits Times; p. 8, Patrick Keith archives (both photos); p. 17, Media Masters archives; p. 26, The New Straits Times (both photos); p. 28, Media Masters archives; p. 40, The New Straits Times; p. 44, The New Straits Times; p. 56, The New Straits Times; p. 62, The New Straits Times; p. 68, The New Straits Times; p. 75, The New Straits Times; p. 78, The New Straits Times; p. 86, The New Straits Times; p. 96, Media Masters archives; p. 102, The New Straits Times; p. 104, Media Masters archives; p. 112, The New Straits Times; p. 125, The New Straits Times; p. 134, Singapore National Heritage Board (top photo); p. 134, The New Straits Times (bottom photo); p. 136. Media Masters archives (both photos); p. 139, Singapore National Heritage Board; p. 150, Singapore National Heritage Board; p. 158, The New Straits Times (all photos); p. 166, The New Straits Times; p. 173, Singapore National Heritage Board (both photos); p. 177, Singapore National Heritage Board (both photos); p. 180, Singapore National Heritage Board; p. 193, The New Straits Times; p. 196, Singapore National Heritage Board; p. 198, The New Straits Times.

Newspaper headline cuttings forming montages are reproduced with the kind permission of The New Straits Times (KL).

Eight dead and in new rioting

SINGAPORE 'DANGER

Singapore is out

By FELIX ABISHEGANADEN: Kuala Lumpur, Monday

SINGAPORE today separated from Malaysia following an amendment to the Constitution approved unanimously by both Houses of P

Lee gi a hint:

ALTERNATIVE ARRANGEMENT

could b partitio

SINGAPORE, M SINGAPORE'S Prime Mr. Lee Kuan Yew, la spoke of the possibility

Razak hits Lee: 'Dangerous and mischievous'

SHOCK TAXES

on profits from tin mining

Lee: A Malaysian Malaysia is essential

SINGAPORE, Friday.

SINGAPORE'S Premier, Mr. Lee Kuan Yew, tonight stressed the tance of creating a Malay and called on political realities of the this nation.

Daho pl is f

Partiti I would be the last ma to sugge that: Lee

The Straits Tim

FRIDAY, JUNE 11, 1965

AP should note there is limit to our patience'

Kuan Yew ungrateful man, says Khir Joha

★ From Page 1

blackening the name of the Central overnment over-seas"

ore Prime Minister "showed himself teful man by the famed "I" name overseas".

fficient proof to had

LEE: S PUMPIN COMMUN IDEAS

● From Page One

enu to Lee: out in the

e in power? I wish him

ck, I'm a tired man, but...

he people won't have him—Tengku

Truth will out says Lee

People in Singapor more interested in making Malaysia a success, says Lee

Razak winds up: PAP stands or Partition and Perish

'Put Lee away to sob up or exclude S'pore

THER OF THESE MEASURES L ENSURE PEACE D HARMONY IN OUR UNTRY, TAN URGES GOVT

QUOTE

Tengku Abdul Rahman never thought of Mr. Lee Kuan Yew or his party as the enemy from within...they are not